D2C Growth
Revolution

D2C Growth Revolution

The No. 1 Growth Strategy for Consumer Brands

STEFAN

RAMERSHOVEN

IMPRESSUM

A catalog record of this book is available at the National Library of Germany.

All inquiries should be made to:
hello@d2cgrowthrevolution.com
For further information and bonus material visit:
https://www.*d2cgrowthrevolution.com*

Creator: Stefan Ramershoven
ISBN: 979-8-5547875-6-0 (paper back)

Disclaimer:
The advice provided in this publication is general advice only. It has been prepared without taking into account your objectives, financial situation, or business needs. Before acting on this advice you should consider the appropriateness of the advice, having regard to your own objectives, financial situation, and business needs. To the maximum extent of the law the author disclaims all responsibility and liability to any person, arising directly or indirectly from any person taking or not taking action based on the information in this publication.

This book contains links to websites, which are out of the author's sphere of influence and subject to change.

To caffeine and sugar, my companions through many long nights of writing.

To my parents, who raised me to follow my dreams and supported me every step of the way.

To my friends and to the woman I chose to spend the rest of my life with, without your unwavering support, sacrifice, and belief in me, this work would not have been possible.

I dedicate this book to all those who will ignore my warning and soon be left without brands to advertise for.

Table of Contents

Preface

Why Me? Why Now? Why This?

Dear colleague,

Picking up this book was a very smart choice. It will be an eye-opener and just may change your entire perspective on the concept of marketing.

Since you probably don't know me, you might be wondering why you should read this book or listen to anything I have to say. Well, let me tell you who I am and why I wrote it in the first place.

I am a growth marketer and digital expert and the CEO of Kjero. I founded the company when I was still at university and have been running it successfully for almost a decade. Today, it is one of the leading providers of direct-to-consumer marketing solutions in Germany, Austria, and Switzerland, working in cooperation with some of the world's leading CPG and consumer electronics brands (Nestlé, Henkel,

Beiersdorf, Wilkinson, Mars, Melitta, Dr. Oetker, Bosch, Philips, etc.). I have co-founded several other companies since then, have been mentioned in several publications and books, and was notably on the Forbes 30 under 30 list. I should be nothing but happy with myself, the world, and my achievements. However, the truth is that I have grown increasingly frustrated with brands, their managers and marketers, and the agencies they are consulting.

Why?

You have probably heard this before: Not just one, but countless indicators show that traditional brands in FMCG, as we know them, are on a clear downward trajectory (if not, you will soon understand what I mean).

Surprisingly, brands and the agencies they are "consulting" seem to simply ignore all the signs. They pretend not to notice anything.

I understand very well why agencies overlook these changes or, in fact, use them to keep selling their sh**. However, it utterly baffles me that brands, or rather the people standing behind them, still blindly follow their "consultants' advice."

Is this ignorance, the inability to change, or blind trust in such "consultants" who allow outdated and indoctrinated growth models to be artificially kept alive to maximize their own profits? It might even be caused by the faulty translation of goals within an organization.

Whatever the cause, a misguided focus on antiquated KPIs and meaningless proxies in advertising that give no true indication of brand success is essentially the basis for the creeping deaths of brands.

This highly dysfunctional marketing strategy leads many traditional brands to throw most of their marketing budget into a bottomless pit, thereby creating a toxic environment for the brands, the agencies, and the consumers.

If these brands keep going this way, they will all be gone sooner or later.

Instead of ignoring recent developments and trying to combat losses through increased spending and bigger advertisement campaigns, brands need to take a step back. They need to refocus. They need to understand the current trends and what really makes a brand successful. They need to understand why awareness alone does not translate into sales anymore.

Something must be done right now to stop all our favorite brands—the ones we grew up with—from disappearing.

With this book, I aim to lift the veil that conceals the truth from brands. I desire to cure their blindness and shed light on what is really going on in the world.

I did not simply write this book for brand managers, managing directors, CMOs, CEOs, and all those in marketing and sales departments.

No, this is also aimed at media agencies, publishers, and all those in the media-landscape that profit from and depend on the success and marketing expenditure of brands. If brands fall, they will also follow.

In this book, I offer a new point of view, one that will help you to better understand how brand value is created. If the flaws in the system are not realized, not only the brands but their entire circle of influence will disappear.

I strongly urge you to read this book. The entire book. From the first page to the last. Every chapter builds on the previous one. Even if you are tempted to think you already have a good grip on a topic and know everything about it, do not skip any parts. Chances are you will miss a crucial aspect and, in turn, won't be able to complete the picture and make sense of the whole.

Don't get me wrong here. I didn't write this book simply to tattle on all your wrongdoings. No, I want to help you all and offer a new perspective, a new approach, to lead you toward sustainable marketing success.

It is not that all you do is pointless and needs to stop right now. However, what you do is not enough. In order to survive and to achieve sustainable growth, you need the ultimate method. I will give you a simple yet highly effective solution to all your problems.

Sincerely,
Stefan Ramershoven

P.S. This is not a "get rich quick" book. However, this will work for all industrious brands.

P.P.S. If, however, your product is a shelf warmer—a dead product—none of what I have to offer will help you. Bad products will not sell, and good advertising will only kill them faster.

Introduction

The slow death of consumer goods

"Today, one can't simply launch a creative TV campaign to then sit down, wait and see. [...] At the same time, one can't simply ask how to create awareness but how to convert that awareness into demand for one's own products."

—Luis di Como
Senior Vice President of Global Media Unilever

A Bleak Future

There are dark times ahead of us. Traditional brands are slowly dying. The biggest players in the industry are below average in terms of growth. Brands are being dropped by retailers left and right. They are losing their spots on the shelves. If nothing changes, if we don't change, they will all be gone by the turn of the century.

You might not believe me when I tell you this. However, I am certainly not the only one with this grim premonition. Bain & Company expects the organic growth of brands in the FMCG sector to keep declining and so does the Financial Times. In 2009, Jim Collins had written a book about the fall of the mighty. The Harvard Business Review blog called this phenomenon "the slow death of the FMCG marketer." Finally, the COVID-19 pandemic has made it painfully clear to all brands that they are far too reliant on retail.

Kraft Heinz is the perfect example of what I mean here. I remember growing up with Heinz Ketchup. The dinner table was not complete without it. The brand has been around for ages—150 years to be more precise. It was founded in 1869, but by 2019, it was on the verge of extinction. Depending too heavily on outdated marketing strategies and underestimating the increasing pressure from upcoming competition and retailers had pretty much sealed its fate. In February 2019, the brand faced a $12.6 billion loss and cut its dividend by 36%. This brand, like many others, failed to observe and adjust to the changes in our environment.

Retailers are developing their own in-house brands and decreasing the shelf space of the big players. These retailers now hold a unique position where they can threaten to drop brands from their shelves entirely if they do not offer a price the retailers see fit. This is a threat that brands should take seriously, especially in light of recent developments. Too many varied brands are available, and shelf space in brick and mortar stores is limited. In fact, one of the biggest retailers in Germany, Edeka, has already dropped Heinz Ketchup. Following a disagreement on pricing, the grocery retailer simply decided that people liked the in-house brand just as much and they didn't need Heinz anymore.

Heinz is not the only one this has happened to. Traditional brands are too dependent on retailers. In Germany, Nestlé wasn't restocked by Edeka for months until they came to an agreement. Unilever was equally threatened by Kaufland, and 480 products were even taken out of the shelves. In Belgium, Colruyt, a retailer, temporarily took 18 Nestlé products down. Due to a price dispute, one of Nestlé's breakfast brands was pulled from Woolworths shelves. The same thing happened to Mars Petcare products. Walmart had dropped brands such as Glad and Hefty for a while. Tesco has reduced its stock of individual brands by more than half in the past five years. Even more concerning, 75% of Lidl's stock already comprises store brands. These are tough times we are living in.

There is another way to do business—one that avoids unnecessary dependencies. Born-digital brands are pioneering new strategies that cut retailers out of the picture entirely by directly catering to consumers.

These so-called direct-to-consumer brands are changing consumers' expectations of what a brand is supposed to be and do. They are encroaching on the playing field and further increasing the pressure put on traditional brands.

Adjusting to changes has proven difficult for FMCG conglomerates. They try to combat their losses through the acquisition of other smaller brands, forgetting all the while to adapt themselves. Customer-focused innovation needs to be at the center of any strategy. Otherwise, there will be no future.

Here is the Problem—A Gap

During consultations and discussions with brands and their managers, I am often told that even though their latest campaign had impressive results in terms of reach and creating awareness, the products did not sell. They ask how this is possible and demand an explanation. To me, it is painfully obvious why this is happening. It is the systemic problem in today's approach to marketing—a gap between awareness and sales uplift.

Brands can no longer sit back and relax while relying on their name and status alone. Resting on one's laurels is not an option in this highly competitive advertising battlefield. Short-term fixes are not going to save them this time around. Strategies such as increase in ad pressure and reach via TV commercials and other mass media are not sufficient anymore. The FMCG market is fully saturated. All brands and products claim to be the best and no 10 to 30-second TV commercial is going to convince me, or anyone else, that one brand is better than another. In addition to that, the more pressure we put on a consumer, the less likely they are to pay attention.

We need something better, something stronger. We need to appeal to our consumers on a different level and create a deeper connection—one that is not based on superficial brand messages distributed via mass media.

Direct-to-consumer brands are already on the right path. Some retailers have also realized what is going on and have turned their in-house brands into consumer magnets, such as dm did with Langhaar Mädchen and Seinz. These are exclusive brands that obtained the top shelf space originally held by traditional brands.

Thanks to the coronavirus crisis, some big brands have started to realize this and shift their focus. The front runner among them is Kraft Heinz.

> *In the future, this channel will be incredibly powerful to get closer to our consumers, get insight, and take learnings to the rest of our business.*
>
> Jean-Phillipe Nier
> Head of E-commerce UK&I, The Kraft Heinz Company

In this book, I will answer a question that is self-evident in my eyes. I will explain in detail why exactly all of this is happening, where the gap originates from, and how to efficiently bridge it.

We will begin with environmental influences and cover the internal mechanics of brands as well as the changing needs and desires of consumers as all these aspects need to be considered. Most importantly, I will give you a way out. If you understand the why and the how, the solution will become evident as a combination of traditional and modern logic is required to create a fresh marketing and growth model.

We will begin with external influences on brands:
- current trends that offset the traditional value creation model of brands

Then, we will look at the internal mechanics of a brand:
- What makes a brand valuable to consumers and which consumers are the most profitable to brands

From here, we will move on to the modern consumer:
- How consumers make purchase decisions and how brands should evolve
- Why brands should strive for loyalty and how to attain/retain it
- A simple means to improve image, increase sales/growth, and take control

How all of this can be made possible:
- What opportunities digital and technological advancements really bring
- How young/agile brands got the upper hand and what to learn from them

Finally,
- How the new and the old can be combined for a new means of brand growth.

Let's get started!

1. Changing Environments and Current Trends

Why the traditional value-creation model no longer works

"Learning and innovation go hand in hand. The arrogance of success is to think that what you did yesterday will be sufficient for tomorrow."

—C. William Pollard
Former Chairman and CEO of ServiceMaster Co.

"Innovation needs to be part of your culture. Consumers are transforming faster than we are, and if we don't catch up, we're in trouble."

—Ian Schafer
Co-Founder/CEO of Kindred
& Founder/Former CEO of DeepFocus.

"Today's chief executive faces a baffling dilemma. Change gets costlier every day, yet not changing can be costlier still."

—John D. Louth
McKinsey Quarterly

Historical Marketing

It used to be fairly simple to be successful as a brand in the FMCG industry. Let me give you an example of one of the first big advertising stunts to clarify what I mean. In the 1920s, Edward Bernays only needed a small match (literally) to ignite a firestorm. He grabbed people's attention by getting young women to smoke in public. Everybody was talking about it. Outrage erupted across the United States, and within weeks, the sale of cigarettes more than doubled. However, things have changed since then. It has grown increasingly difficult to grab people's attention. A match is no longer enough. Today, you need nothing short of a wildfire. To explain why this is the case, we first need to look at how brand value used to be created earlier.

Ever since the 1950s, all one needed to grow was to make sure that as many people as possible knew about their brand and would recognize it on the shelves of a retail store. To ensure this, advertisements were aired on television, preferably during prime time, published in newspapers, or even distributed as eye-catching posters on busy street corners. Further, they made sure the product was available everywhere.

Developing economies aided the growth of FMCG companies and brands, which led to rising returns. Booming brands fulfilled consumer demand and could ask for higher prices, while retailers had limited ability to bargain.

Until recently, this kind of value-creation model worked well enough, but this is no longer the case. Growth rates are dropping, and company success is stagnating, even shrinking. Why?

To be more precise, the value creation model in FMCG used to look something like this:

- (Premium) products were introduced into the mass market, coupled with brand building and product innovation, which were meant to secure a considerable advantage over weaker and no-name brands and guarantee stable growth.

- Relationships with retailers opened mass trade opportunities and gave companies superior access to consumers and broad distribution while limiting the competition.

- The creation of new market categories and insertion of oneself into developing markets, as well as the consumers' inflating incomes, led to a revenue growth of 75% over the past 10 years.

Today, consumer behaviors and needs are changing and so should the channels used for advertising. To stay on top of the game in FMCG, companies need to reconsider their dependence on mass brands and channels. Growth is no longer a natural occurrence, and these three bullet points aren't cutting it anymore.

Agile models with a focus on the relevance a brand has for the consumer are required. But before we get into detail about that, let's find out why this old model, which has been successful for so long, is starting to fail us.

Consumers:
Changing Needs and New Power

Several trends and developments now disrupt this long-standing and, until recently, very successful value creation model. A major part of this owes to the fact that consumers are not what they used to be. We can't define them the same way we did a decade ago. They are changing and diversifying.

As mentioned before, the FMCG industry used to strongly focus on the mass market. Reaching as many people as possible through brand building ad campaigns was the major goal and, for a great deal, still is. This, unfortunately, is not a suitable approach for today's consumers.

New gen

The consumers born between 1980 and 1995—in other words, the millennials—are considerably different from the generations that came before them, especially in terms of their wants and needs. But don't underestimate their impact: according to the UNO, they make up 30% of the world population today. This generation is very careful with what and where they buy their products and how much they spend on them. According to McKinsey's research, millennials are almost four times more likely than baby boomers to avoid buying products from "the big food companies." Why should they buy Barilla pasta if the retailer's in-house brand pasta tastes the same and is sold at half the price? Brand loyalty is hard to come by these days. In fact, market research has shown that every third consumer prefers to try new things when it comes to foods and household goods. New brands are often considered to be superior, more original, and of a higher quality.

Then, there is Gen Z—those born after 1995. This generation is active on different social media platforms, and they use their smartphones more readily to make a purchase. Also, they are less likely to be influenced by TV commercials; only 21% use them as a source of information while making purchasing decisions. They also stream more clips online—an average of 68 per day. But most importantly, they are very value-driven consumers. This generation is interested in the environment and in equality and is more likely to buy from brands that do so as well.

These new generations are a tough crowd for brands to cater to.

Organic and sustainable

Another change in consumer behaviors can be noticed in the areas of health and lifestyle, which is not exclusively limited to but originates from the new generations. Talk on living and eating healthier has grown louder over the years and is becoming increasingly prevalent in all aspects of life.

Recently, people have started to change their conduct, especially their shopping behavior. In particular, foods now need to be green and organic. They should be sugar and fat-free with no gluten, pesticides, or any kind of chemicals, and they most certainly should not be genetically engineered. Eggs need to come from free-range chicken, and cheese should be vegetarian or even vegan. Fresh food is also preferred. Thus, this is not an easy market for the packaged food industry.

Information and trust

The main difference between these new kinds of consumers and previous generations is that young people do a lot of research. They generally don't believe what companies say about themselves. Advertisements are generally perceived to be embellished and overly positive ideas filled with unachievable body images. No company would ever openly and honestly say anything negative about themselves. In fact, a study by Trinity Mirror and Ipsos in the UK found that 42% of the respondents distrusted brands and an astonishing 69% distrusted brand advertising. Among millennials, this number was as high as 89% and these figures are on the rise. The graph clearly shows a general decline in trust in brands. Instead, young consumers turn to their peers to find out about brands and their products They trust in their friends' opinions, not in advertising messages. Most people would even trust a stranger's online review over a brand commercial or as much as a friend's recommendation.

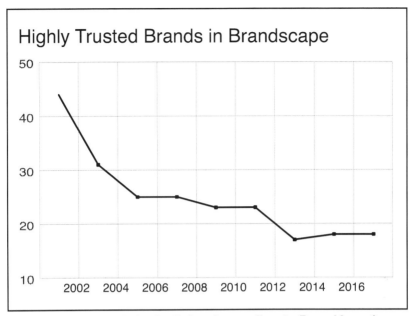

Trust in brands is declining (according to BrandAsset)

However, this influence only applies to genuine friends and acquaintances, not influencers and the like, who have the effect of a media channel. While this might sound devastating, it could be a great opportunity as well, but we will get into more detail on that later on in the book.

The shift in attention

This brings us to the biggest problem the traditional value creation model is facing today: Advertisements don't receive a lot of attention anymore, if any. Even if the advertisement targets one consumer directly, the product is cheap or on promotion, and it fulfills all the criteria the customer could have, it is still not guaranteed that the advertisement will be noticed. This is because people have learned to ignore them.

People pick the most relevant information and pay no attention to the rest. Looking at everything on a website and trying to take it all in would be far too time-consuming. Rather, they only focus on the things they are interested in. This is a process known as selective attention, where people look for something specific and ignore everything else, like advertisements. According to a study by the Nielsen Norman Group, people do this 65% of the time.

When it comes to TV commercials, not even those who still watch television and have not yet switched to streaming services, such as Netflix, pay attention during commercial breaks. Instead, they divert their focus to their mobile phones and check social media to find out what their friends are up to. They shift their attention to more relevant things.

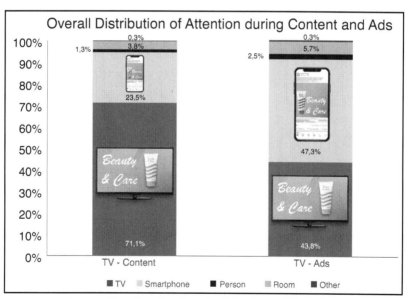

**How attention is diverted during ad breaks
(according to Andy Ford)**

According to the AdScanner and A1 IPTV Panel, 15.4% of the audience switches channels within the first ten seconds of a commercial. This number does not even include all those who simply walk away or switch to other devices during the break. The graphic above gives you some more details on that.

Not only televised commercials but online advertisements are also impacted. Banner ads, for example, are purposefully blocked out with ad-blockers or unconsciously through banner blindness. While the first banner ad twenty years ago had an astonishing click-through rate (CTR) of 44%, today, this number has an average of below 1%. More like 0.1%. And this rate does not even adjust for fat finger clicks, which occur when people accidentally click on ads.

This lack of attention has to do with the immense pressure advertisements and other stimulations put on us. We are constantly surrounded by them. In fact, we receive between 4000 and 10,000 advertising and sales messages a day. That's far too much information to process. In other words, it causes information overload. Therefore, people try to filter out and only focus on what is deemed relevant or important to them. Ads usually draw the short straw in this equation. Even in cases where the message is somehow absorbed unconsciously, the consumer will most likely not be able to recall it.

You might think this obstacle can be bypassed by disguising advertisements as content, but this is not the case. In fact, research has shown that ads that are not properly labeled as such and only later turn out to be advertisements have a severe, negative effect on the sympathy and trust afforded to the company and brand behind it, which in turn, affects sales. People just don't like to be duped.

On the other hand, an increase in pressure and impressions would not be a viable option either as this would only result in a general decrease in attention paid to advertisements. We are already being bombarded by too much information as, not just advertisements, but a whole multitude of other elements are competing for our attention, such as WhatsApp messages, push notifications, social media feeds and many more. Compare this to walking into a room where twenty people are trying to talk to you at once. You probably won't be able to understand even a single one.

This brings us to the second major change we are facing today, which you might have guessed, is the instruments and tools we use.

Changing Channels
and Technologies

A substantial number of new channels have appeared in addition to the original TV, print, and radio trilogy, for example, the previously mentioned banner ads. However, the biggest changes and challenges we are facing today came with Web 2.0, which opened an infinite number of possibilities for consumer and brands, making it increasingly hard to keep up.

Two-way communication

One such possibility is the increased intimacy between FMCG brands and consumers. Nowadays, manufacturers, their brands, and any information about them are just a click away. Consumers can easily learn about and get in touch with brands and their representatives. The opposite is also true: brands can access a vast amount of data on and from their customers now. Unfortunately, one or both options are often overlooked. Consumer data is not used properly, nor is its value realized and appreciated. Customers state when and how they want to receive information and products and of what kind they should be, and they expect brands to understand and remember their needs to improve their experience.

Data: collect, store, transfer, and analyze

Modern technologies and digitalization have created the possibility for massive amounts of data to be collected, stored, and transferred, the extent of which is almost unimaginable and steadily increasing.

In 2016, as much data was produced as in the entire history of humankind till 2015. This has led to a multitude of problems: collection of too much data, useless data, wrong data, and low-value data. Also, new rules have been put in place to regulate data collection and privacy, such as the GDPR.

However, data is most valuable for brands if it is collected firsthand, in real-time, and directly from the source. Instead of relying on intermediaries to collect data, brands should collect their own actionable data.

With this kind of data as the basis for decision-making and forming marketing strategies, you can minimize expenses and maximize return. It can help you understand how consumers engage with and respond to your marketing campaign. This, in turn, allows you to adjust and improve strategies and even predict a customer's future wants with a high level of accuracy. Most importantly, collecting consumer data enables you to market directly to the people most likely to engage with you. By ignoring this possibility, many great opportunities would be missed or go unnoticed entirely. We will go into more detail on this aspect later.

Fragmentation

Currently, there is a whole bunch of different social media platforms, such as Facebook, Snapchat, Pinterest, Instagram, TikTok, and LinkedIn. People from various age groups with diverse interests tend to prefer different platforms. In fact, every generation seems to have its own. For example, Instagram and Pinterest are mostly used by women, and Snapchat is more popular among school kids and teenagers, while teens are abandoning Facebook. The platform has seen a drop from 71% to only 51% in this demographic. Social media marketing would have been so much easier if your audience used a single, joint platform, but this is not the case.

In order to capitalize on fragmentation, you not only need to know who your target audience is but also on which platform to find them. That is not all, it's also getting harder to reach your target audience on individual platforms. Just take a look at the drop of organic reach on Facebook.

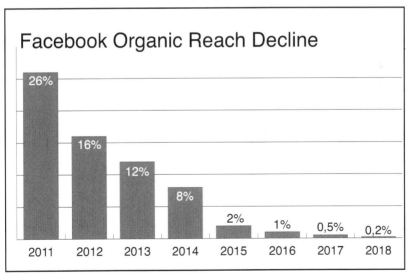

Organic reach is declining

However, you should not overdo it either. Too much infiltration of the consumers' personal domain will only backfire. Posting too much as well as posting the wrong content on the wrong platform can have a negative impact on your brand image. So, you should be cautious when, where, and how you post content to social media. In general, social media should not be used as a message board but rather to build relations and engage with your target audience.

On top of that, social media allows users to become channels themselves as they can create and share content across the globe. I am not solely talking about influencers with millions of followers. Every person using a platform has their own circle of influence. Even if one's audience comprises only five other people, everyone has the potential to turn viral overnight. They are no longer passive receivers of messages but creators and producers; some even call them prosumers. This is not something you need to be overly concerned about but, instead, something you can use to your advantage, especially considering consumers' need for real-world proof from real-life people to believe marketing messages from brands. Aligning advertising claims and real-life actions is something brands and businesses can no longer fake.

Online shopping

Another big change and a new trend is the rise of e-commerce giants such as Amazon, eBay, and Zalando. They attract consumers in all categories and have a huge impact on them. They offer competitive prices, wide selection, and more convenience. This has consequences on online as well as offline FMCGs, especially considering the rapid expansion of these e-commerce giants. Some are contemplating opening or have already opened brick-and-mortar locations, which may turn into a serious threat for retailers and, in turn, for the brands depending on these retailers. To get a glimpse of what that could mean, we need only look at how Amazon has affected the books and publishing industry or the effect e-commerce giants such as Alibaba had on FMCG retailing in China.

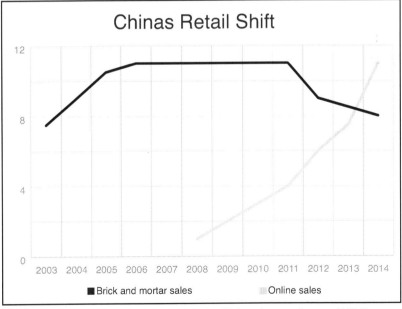

The steep rise of online retail in China (according to WSJ)

By providing publishers with a way to transition into the digital age and offering them a new stream of revenue, Amazon put a lot of bookstores out of business. Today, the company holds more than half of the online book market in the US. This is starting to put pressure on publishers as they allow authors to self-publish and bypass publishers altogether. Some have even begun to worry about what is going to happen to authors once Amazon has eliminated publishers.

This doesn't have to be a bad thing. In fact, it could be an opportunity for you as a brand to sidestep retailers altogether. In fact, more FMCG brands are launching innovative e-commerce concepts and going the direct-to-consumer way.

Only brands that are agile and forward-thinking enough to identify new opportunities and adapt will succeed. In order to succeed, consumer demand and brand loyalty are required.

Market Disruptions

Driven by the trends and changes already discussed, the market has changed considerably as well. As previously hinted, changing consumer needs and the available technologies have created an ideal environment for small brands and start-ups.

Hyper-focused (small) brands

There has been an explosion of hyper-focused brands, which concentrate on the younger generation's favorite form of marketing—digital and personal—and allow these brands to grow quickly. These small brands often go unnoticed by the bigger players. They sell their products online and outside the conventional brands' field of vision. Those who do notice the direct-to-consumer brands, such as the head of global categories of the healthcare giant GlaxoSmithKline (GSK), Carlton Lawson, consider small players with close customer relationships to be more of a threat than the likes of Unilever or P&G.

These small brands have not gone unnoticed by retailers either who view them as an opportunity to differentiate themselves from their competition and propel their surplus because these brands usually offer high-end products and do not tend to hold promotions; thus, these brands receive more shelf space, and this, in turn, boosts the brand's growth. Also, since these small brands usually start as direct-to-consumer brands, they already have a community—a fan base. Retails can also profit from this community being activated. Further, small brands tend to gravitate towards categories with high margins, emotional engagement, possibilities to outsource the value chain, low shipment costs, and minimum regulation.

This is true for most FMCG sectors but especially for beauty products. According to McKinsey, in color cosmetics, small brands already hold 10 % of the market and are growing four times faster than others. This is further reinforced using digital marketing.

An extraordinary amount of user-generated and beauty-related content is available on social media. The forerunners in this sector are leading the way and many others are slowly starting to follow.

Peddlers turf war

A different development that is driving change in the market is e-commerce, which is disrupting the retail business model. Retail stores are put under further pressure by discounters, who take up an average of 20% in any market they infiltrate.

Retailers are trying to diminish some of this pressure by filling a major portion of their shelves, especially the best spots, with their own in-house brand. But this means the few, less favorable spots on the shelves are left for your company and brands. On top of this, two-thirds of consumers put the same level of trust in those in-house brands and perceive them to be of equal quality as branded goods. Further, most consumers do not even notice if a brand is missing from retailers' shelves. Since retailers are becoming tougher trading partners with more aggressive goals, they may take drastic measures to reach these goals. Thus, it may not be very smart to keep relying on them too much or for too long.

The following graph puts this into perspective. Within five years, brand product sales increased by 7.4% from $236.1 to $253.6 (billion). Private label sales, on the other hand, increased by 41% from $43.1 to $60.8 (billion).

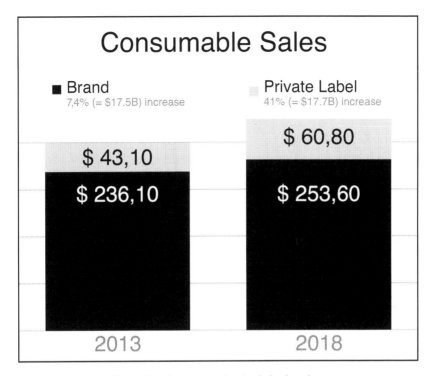

Consumable Sales

■ Brand
7,4% (= $17.5B) increase

Private Label
41% (= $17.7B) increase

$ 43,10

$ 60,80

$ 236,10

$ 253,60

2013

2018

Brand sales vs. private label sales
(according to PLMA/Nielsen)

Native competitors

Another development that hinders the success of the original value creation model for FMCG brands is the rise of local competition. Developing markets have been a consistent source of potential growth, but local competitors will also be contenders for this growth, much more so now than in the past. This development is forcing brands to rethink their centralized control system because markets are developing in new and unforeseen ways. For example, the FMCG markets in China and Indonesia are growing by approximately 9% a year, but big brands are losing up to 5% of their share in these markets.

This can partly be accredited to the fact that, even though the middle class is booming, their mass media is fragmented, and their infrastructure is weak. In addition, most of these would-be buyers may be purchasing a brand for the first time. Since local competitors are already familiar with and have a better understanding of the natives' wants and needs, they are at a clear advantage here. And as niches are becoming even smaller and more specified, products and advertising aimed at the masses won't cut it for much longer. This does not mean, however, that it is impossible for big, global brands to employ the same strategy. For example, The Coca-Cola Company introduced the Zico Coconut Water brand in India, and Unilever created Hijab Fresh moisturizer.

Consultant or trader

An additional major change that has occurred in the marketplace in recent years is the shift in the focus and purpose of media agencies. While they had started out as simple mediators and facilitators, they soon realized they could profit from offering consultations on advertising and marketing. However, since these agencies do not merely get paid by those trying to advertise a product or service but also by those providing the channel, this creates a conflict of interest.

With the increase in available channels, media agencies began to focus increasingly on planning, processing, and procuring, turning them into key players in the sale and distribution of advertising inventory. Due to the merging of smaller agencies into huge international media holdings, processes and pricing have become increasingly opaque. The resulting oligopolies hold uniquely powerful positions, which allow agencies to buy airtime at disproportionate volumes of discounts and pressure channels into offering additional discounts. On the other end of the spectrum, these agencies then sell them to advertisers with high surcharges. The intentions of these agencies are no longer centered around consulting but instead on maximizing profit from trade.

Because of this focus on profit, they neglect to take changes in the mediascape into account. They make the most profit by selling airtime for TV commercials; therefore, other kinds of advertisements are hardly considered. Oftentimes, these agencies simply lack the ability to look beyond their immediate sphere of influence and thus, do not comprehend the possibilities available today. An increasingly complex value creation chain is adding to the inability of agencies to offer counsel to either marketers or channels. The rising fragmentation and diversification have passed them by, and they are simply not able to grasp the situation anymore. Fragmentation has annihilated any unified currency the advertising market had and yet, they still focus on reach—a metric utterly insignificant in today's day and age. We will get back to this later.

A lot has changed; in fact, hardly anything is the same as it was just a few decades ago. In the next chapter, we will look at what exactly these developments mean for brands and their companies and how they affect brand loyalty and, consequently, earnings. But before we go there, let's recap the main points of our discussion so far.

Recap:
A Comparison of Then and Now

For further clarity, before we move on, let's look at the above-mentioned disruptive trends and the traditional value creation model side by side.

1. The first step towards being successful was introducing a premium product into the mass market, building up a brand and continuously innovating the product.

But, today, most of the growth in the industry stems from niches, not the mass. People have begun to resist mass brands, thus offering an advantage to small brands and local competition. Instead of paying attention to ads, consumers would rather consult others to find the best product. There is less trust in and, due to our overstimulated brains, no recollection of any advertisements that consumers pass by unconsciously, even if they are the target audience in the labyrinth of channels.

2. The second part was ensuring good relations with retailers since they offered access to a broad range of consumers.

This situation is changing because e-commerce and discounters are increasingly pressurizing these retailers, and they, in turn, are starting to divert some of that pressure on to you. They are beginning to focus on their own in-house brands instead of your brand, which might entice them to drop you from their shelves entirely without the consumers even noticing.

3. Finally, creating new market categories and entering developing markets was a method to boost a company's growth further.

Competition in this area is continuing to grow stronger. Small and local companies, as well as direct-to-consumer brands, are better equipped to quickly and continually adjust to development and identify specific ideals of these new markets.

Of course, the impact of these disruptive trends vary by category. However, I am not trying to say that what you, your company, and your brand are doing today is completely wrong. Neither am I saying that there is no hope. But there is change, and it can no longer be ignored. The mass market is corroding. Consumers are continually focusing on smaller niches on which no data is available. Those who don't adjust are likely to soon be replaced by in-house brands or others that are strategically better equipped. The traditional growth model is no longer working properly since competition is increasing and brand loyalty is starting to sound like a myth. Fragmented channels and audiences make reach and pressure pointless measures. Media agencies are no longer consulting with a focus on the brands' or channels' best interests but their own. They have lost the ropes in this business. These agencies simply do not know enough about the diverse kinds of channels and KPIs available. The focus needs to shift.

These are only a few of the big trends that could get any idle brand in trouble. Lighting a match and hoping for the fire to spread is no longer an option. The world has become flame(ad)-resistant. So I have just one question for you: How do you plan on starting a wildfire without using a match?

2. A Debilitating Gap

Brand awareness rates

don't translate to sales anymore

"Build something 100 people love, not something 1 million people kind of like."

—*Brian Chesky*
Co-founder of Airbnb

"Your brand advocates are more valuable than any advertisement you could ever buy."

—*Dave Kerpen*
Co-founder and Chairman of Likeable Media

Success Held Hostage

In the last chapter, we talked about the big trends and changes in the world of consumers, technology, and the market and about how these external influences are obscuring the traditional value creation model—a model that focuses on the mass market via centralized channels. In short, the root cause of a major obstacle was described. In this chapter, we will look at the problem from a different angle. Namely, we will observe how these trends have affected consumers' perception of brands. We will see how by leaving crucial things to chance, consumers are lost to the competition.

A brand lives and falls at the feet of its consumers. How well you fare in the market against your direct and indirect competition is based largely on the image attached to your brand, your product performance, and how it can be differentiated from others. Consumers hold brand success hostage. Just because consumers acknowledge your brand's existence does not imply they are automatically persuaded to buy the products. It should be crystal clear by now that it is becoming increasingly difficult to reach target audiences effectively and that the competition is multiplying. Having a product of superior quality with excellent ingredients and a decent price is still insufficient to guarantee a favorable outcome. You need to appeal to your consumers on a different level and create trust and a lasting relationship. Otherwise, you will not stand a chance in this cutthroat environment.

Genuine or Superficial:
The Brand Triad

To clarify this last statement, let me introduce to you the theoretical model of the brand triad, which you might have heard of before.

The brand triad, as the name implies, consists of three parts. You can picture it as a funnel that people go through in order to become brand users. First, there is **awareness** followed by **affinity** and, lastly, **utilization**. These three cornerstones can show you how your brand is set-up, where its strengths and weaknesses are located, and how your target audience perceives it. Therefore, the brand triad is a tool that allows an assessment of the efficiency of your marketing strategy and communication. How does your brand perform in comparison to others, and is there potential for optimization? To answer this, we should take a closer look at these three individual aspects.

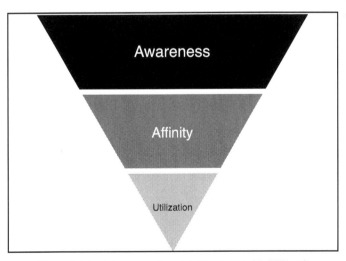

Brand triad (according to Prof. Dr. K. Kilian)

Awareness is obviously the basis the model rests on. Without people who know about your brand's existence, sale is not possible. Thus, a lot of focus is being placed on awareness in the current marketing strategies. There are, as you probably know, two kinds of awareness. The first is called brand recall or top-of-mind awareness, which means that people can recall a brand without receiving any hints. For example, think about the brands that automatically come to mind when you think of mobile phones.

Then, there is brand recognition or aided recall. These are not the first brands people think of, but they can recognize their logos when they see them. A lot of time, money, and effort are invested into this aspect of brand setup. Reaching top-of-mind awareness is the ultimate goal for all brands, but only very few ever reach it.

Here is where the problem lies: while building up fame and awareness is certainly necessary, it is not enough to make your brand a successful and healthy one, especially if only a superficial affiliation is created.

Awareness needs to be charged with sympathy to create users and customers. With every purchase, a conscious or unconscious decision is made that excludes many other possible alternatives. At least when the point of sale is reached, a brand must assert itself against the temptation of buying other products and brands, especially those that are appealing due to their prominent presentation or particularly low prices. Only the brands that manage to create appeal on a personal level and to individuals' sympathies have a higher chance of actually being selected.

Let me put this in numbers for you. If there is no affinity, a brand only has a 4% chance of making a sale, and this 4% can largely be accredited to the price–performance ratio. This is also why so much budget is allotted to brand building. Now, brands are trying to create sympathy and affinity by charging their image with certain values. However, it usually isn't all that simple.

What I mean to convey might become clearer with an example. Have you seen that TV commercial for anti-aging cream? I mean the one with that celebrity and a lot of close-ups of her face. She has absolutely no wrinkles even though she is in her early fifties. You know the one I'm referring to. Which brand was it again?

It could be anyone—Diadermine, Olaz, L'Oréal; they all have the exact same advertisement. The only difference in these kinds of commercials is the brand logo and product design.

> Do you want to see what a generic brand video looks like? Check this out: https://www.d2cgrowthrevolution/ resources#generic-brand-video
> It'shilarious!

How do any of these brands expect to be differentiated from their competition on retail store shelves? There is just no way. If these brands do not create some kind of true sympathy or deep emotional connection with their target audience, they will never be able to outperform their competition. What you need is a high conversion to the second part of the triad, **affinity**.

What do I mean by conversion? Well, it's simple. A healthy brand has a high conversion from awareness to sympathy and, finally, to **utilization**. In other words, a healthy brand has a harmonious brand triad—many people who know the brand, like the brand, and out of these, there are many who actually use the brand's products. If your brand is unhealthy, on the other hand, the opposite is true—it has a dissonant brand triad. There might be a lot of people who know about your brand, but they are indifferent to it. They will most likely choose the products sold by one of your more likable competitors before even considering you.

A communications analysis study among women in Germany, which was conducted by Media Markt Analysen and IPSOS and published in Brigitte (one of the most popular women's magazines in Germany), identified five different conditions a brand triad can be in.

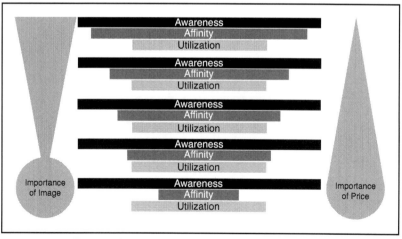

From a healthy to a dissonant brand triad
(according to Media Markt Analysen and IPSOS)

Balanced conversion

Here, the dimension of the affinity potential is the average of awareness and utilization, and there is a smooth transition from one to the other. If your brand triad is in this condition, you are off to a good start. According to the study, in 2012, about 50% of the brands in Germany were in this category.

An example of this would be NIVEA Creme. 84% of the respondents in the previously mentioned study knew it, 47% liked it, and 30% are using it. Miele was known to 96% of the respondents, liked by 67%, and used by 57%.

Weak affinity surplus

In this case, those that the brand appeals to are already users, which is true for 12% of the brands in Germany. While this might, at first glance, appear to be a good thing, it is not. If there is no surplus of sympathizers, little to no growth can be generated.

This, according to the study, is true for C&A as 96% of the women who took part in the study knew about the brand. 60% of them liked the brand and those where the 60% that used it. Also, 96% knew of Dr. Oetker, and 63% liked and used it.

To turn around a situation like this, brands can try to create affinities with new target audiences.

Low utilization

This means that even though many know and like the brand, sales are slow. 15% of brands are in this situation, mostly pricy luxury brands like Chanel. This brand was known by 75% of respondents, 28% liked it, but only 10% actually used it. Also, Lancome had a conversion rate from 55% to 17% to just 5%.

The problem, however, might also be deeply rooted in the gap. We will get back to this in a bit.

Low affinity

In this situation, people are aware of the brand but indifferent to it. These brands are run-of-the-mill and do not stand out. This is a very unfavorable position that 21% of brands in Germany find themselves in. For example, for Bogner, out of 56% of people who know it, only 11% like it, and 5% use it. Also, even though 87% know Olaz, only 27% like it, and 11% use it.

It is not hard to understand that a generic message like in the example mentioned earlier will not create affinity. Instead, brands need to understand their audience and what it is they want and expect from the brand in order to gain their sympathy.

Affinity deficit

There are brands that people buy even though they don't like them. Only 3% of brands in Germany are in this troublesome situation. A good example here is Knorr; 95% of people know it, but even though only 56% like it, 59% buy and use it.

Affinity is an essential connective link between awareness and utilization. According to their textbook definitions, sympathy and affinity are perceived as equivalent to brand building. Then again, what exactly does affinity constitute and what can a brand do to appear more likable? A brand can be charged with values and emotions to conform to the ideals, lifestyle, and expectations of its target audience so that these users can identify themselves to the brand. There is, however, an alternative way to create affinity—building a real relationship and cultivating it. Ideally, these two approaches go hand in hand.

Few brands realize the importance of creating a relationship between consumers and brands. They don't know it's possible and, thus, don't actively try to create an emotional bond with their consumers. Or maybe they believe the artificial affiliation stemming from awareness is sufficient, but it isn't. In fact, research by Brandshare/ Edelman suggest that 90% of consumers wish to have a relationship of appreciation with brands, but only 14% believe they have one such relationship. On the other hand, 80% of consumers believe that brands only have egoistic motives for their interest in them. Fulfilling this desire for a relationship would be highly beneficial for your brand as consumers would then not only be more willing to buy your product but also advocate for it.

Media agencies usually have a different opinion on this topic. They don't realize the value of true relationships between brands and their customers and counsel in a different direction.

This is because relationships don't fit into agencies' traditional KPI models of reach and ad pressure. Instead of aiming for sympathy and, with it, sales, media agencies target declining reach. Brands, in turn, keep spending more money to achieve KPIs that had been established 50 years ago by those very agencies.

This is a systemic problem resulting in higher investments but lower sales. The example mentioned earlier makes it evident that solely focusing on TV commercials and other mass media channels is highly ineffective. To ensure stable and sustainable success for your product and brand, communication strategies need to include a focus on strengthening **affinity** and **sympathy**. Just like in the previously mentioned example of a TV commercial, merely changing the visuals and testimonials or, more plainly, the actress and the brand logo, is not effective. Therefore, it is essential to create an emotional bond and relation between consumers and the brand, one that goes beyond the awareness achieved with commercials on mass media channels.

I see this way too often: brands whose brand triads are characterized by low sympathy are advised to invest in TV and out-of-home advertising by their agencies. This seems to me like a very generic piece of advice—a recording playing on an endless loop.

Seriously! How could that ever really work out? It seems impractical when trying to compete with more successful brands in those channels—brands that are more popular and have a bigger budget.

Let me give you another example. Just recently, I talked to a colleague of mine who is the brand manager of an international cosmetics brand of a global company, and she told me about this new product they are about to launch. The product is not what you would call a straightforward kind of consumer good. Additional information will need to be given on it as its use is not self-evident. Her media agency had advised her to focus the campaign on mass media—TV and YouTube ads to be specific.

You can probably guess what happened—the campaign failed completely. Their budget was gone, and it was too late to run a useful campaign that would truly fit the specific needs of the product.

How could that be, you might wonder. Isn't TV supposed to be a guaranteed success channel? Apparently not!

The advertising pressure on these channels is already way too high. Thus, consumers' attention is shifting towards other more relevant content. On top of that, her brand's triad does not have the best conversion in comparison to others in the same category. As if this was not enough, her budget was way smaller than that of her competition who used the same strategy.

Having all the facts on paper, how could anyone ever expect this to work out? Seriously!

So, here are some takeaways from this above example.

1) Playing with the big boys

If you can't play in the same league as the top spenders of your category, you shouldn't go for mass media channels. Your chances of winning the fight are slim to none, especially when you intend to employ the same strategy on a lower budget.

2) Don't bring a knife to a gunfight

Particularly if your brand triad is not on par with the top players.

3) You cannot sell to a man who isn't listening (W. Bernbach)

Does your product require a more detailed explanation? Then marketing it on a medium that only has passive listeners will be unsuccessful.

The biggest mistake here is the assumption that one needs to make mass media channels the core of the media project and then just randomly build some smaller activities around it when, especially in cases like this, the whole strategy should be changed. Mass channels should be an addition to the core customer-centered campaign.

Therefore, here is some homework for you folks: Find out at which level the conversion rate to sympathy is for your brand (or customers) and how to increase it.

Let's come back to affinity again. It is the filter that brands generally have to go through to reach utilization and sales.

This means that before your brand or your product is ever granted a chance or before it is ever bought and tried out by someone, that person needs the following:

1. to know it exists/be made aware,
2. a cognitive and emotional attraction superior to other available brands, i.e., appeal and sympathy.

Only then will a consumer consider buying and trying the product.

Standing out in a positive way is the strategic key to long-term success and not being displaced by competitors. But getting people to buy and try your product is still not the end of the story. What you really need are loyal repeat customers.

Misguided Focus: The Brand Loyalty Pyramid

There is one major difference between weak and strong brands. To explain this, I will use a second theoretical model. Enter the brand loyalty pyramid. This model goes beyond the brand triad, which shows the necessary steps to take and obstacles to overcome for utilization. The brand loyalty pyramid shows the big differences between brands after that point in time and shows how a brand is made up of different consumer categories. With this model, you can see how healthy a brand is, how well it is faring, if its marketing strategies are working properly, and where problems or potential still exist.

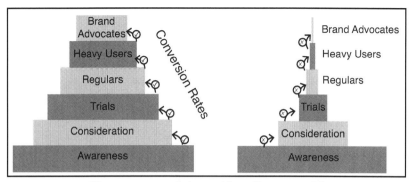

**Strong vs weak brand loyalty pyramid
(according to D.A. Aaker)**

Similar to the brand triad, a successful brand needs a proportional ratio between the different consumer categories and a healthy conversion throughout the pyramid. Sadly, this is not the case for most brands. In fact, most brands suffer from a huge gap between awareness and sales uplift. Where this gap comes from and how to fix it is what we will focus on next. First, we need to make sense of the different categories within the pyramid.

This model also starts with **awareness**. As explained in the brand triad, these are all the people who know about your brand or product.

Then, there is the **consideration** stage. In the brand triad, this was called affinity. These are the people who would consider your brand and evaluate your product for a possible purchase (only if there is sympathy.)

In the **trial** stage are the brand users who have bought and/or tried your product at least once.

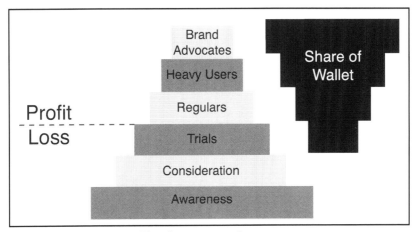

Earnings per category

Up to now, this is pretty similar to the brand triad. Still, stay with me here. I brought this model up for a good reason. Now is where the fun starts.

Real ROIs are generated when users are turned into regular or, even better, loyal customers. The icing on the cake for every brand is its brand advocates. This is the second, upper half of the brand loyalty pyramid.

The term **regulars** is pretty much self-explanatory. These are the brand users who occasionally or regularly buy your brand's products. At this point, usually, the first profit margins are reached. You just need to keep one thing in mind here: These are not loyal customers; they are more than willing to switch to other brands. This is why they would be easy targets for the smart marketing of your competitors except if you are able to turn them into loyals.

Heavy users are devoted repeat customers—they buy your brand a lot. Other brands have a hard time changing the minds and win the favor of these people. In contrast to regulars, these users are very loyal. This loyalty acts like a buffer, shielding them from the advertisements and influence of other brands. That is why, as a brand, you want a whole bunch of this kind of users.

Even better than heavy users are **brand advocates**— the crowning achievement of any brand. They are not just devoted repeat customers but passionate promoters. Advocates actively campaign for your brand to their friends, relatives, and colleagues. Their loyalty is even higher than that of heavy users. Therefore, they are even harder to entice away. These brand advocates do not simply spend more than an average consumer but also bring in an average of three new users to the brand, which means they are about five times as valuable to you. In fact, if you manage to increase the number of heavy users and brand advocates by just 5%, your revenue will increase by between 25% and 100%. This becomes evident when you take into consideration that these two consumer categories hold a majority of the share of wallet. Besides, it is difficult for most companies, especially in the FMCG sector, to profit from one-time buyers as acquisition costs are usually much higher than the profit margin of a single sold product.

Keeping this in mind, the three most common problems a brand with an unhealthy brand loyalty pyramid could be facing are as follows:

1. Even though there is high awareness, there is almost no conversion to consideration. A possible cause for this, aside from lack of affinity, could be that consumers don't understand the product.

2. When a brand can convince many users to try a product but only very few become loyal—i.e., none stick with it—it is highly likely that people are simply more satisfied with the competition. They will switch back to the one they are familiar with after having tried out something new.

3. Sometimes, a brand is able to create regulars but cannot turn them into heavy users and brand advocates. This is often the case with products that are sold at a discount. Here, brands are under constant threat of being replaced as well.

The general dilemma here is the huge gap between awareness and sales uplift. Many brands talk to me about their awesome award-winning campaigns that create great brand awareness, yet their products don't sell.

This was the case for a brand in the supplement industry I recently consulted with. The person in charge bragged about the fantastic work of his media agency and the incredible awareness they generated, but his product was not selling and he simply could not understand what the reason for this could possibly be.

Many readers probably know of this problem or have encountered it before themselves. The cause is usually an unhealthy brand loyalty pyramid and, thus, a weak brand.

This can be very dangerous for individual products as well as for the brand as a whole. In light of this, it is very important to have a concrete marketing strategy for the goal-oriented recruitment of brand users and their development from mere awareness all the way to brand advocacy.

In spite of all this, there is barely a brand out there that has a strategy for the systematic development of the brand according to the brand loyalty pyramid model. This strange phenomenon can be accredited to the fact that brands still follow the outdated doctrines that might have allowed them to grow in the past but no longer do so. Since the beginning of mass advertisements, all brands have followed the same strategy—they invest in the black box media to generate awareness and ad pressure. Based on first-rate—but generic—brand building, this is then supposed to magically and organically develop trialists into satisfied and loyal consumers, who will buy the brand until the end of their days.

These brands all solely focus on a bottom-up strategy. Unfortunately, due to all the trends discussed in chapter one, we know that this is insufficient, even pointless. The hope for an organic sales uplift is slim at best. That should be evident by now.

It is mind-boggling that 90% of advertising budgets are still allocated for mass media channels to gain new customers, especially while considering that 75% of the people buying a product for the first time will only buy it once. To quote Henry Ford, "Half of the investments made in advertising are wasted money. We just don't know which half."

Today, we know, and it is not just half. It is two-thirds. 67.5% of advertising budgets work inefficiently. That being said, it might not be a bad idea to play roulettes and bet your marketing budget on either black or red. Then, you would at least have a 50–50 chance of success.

The rest of the pyramid's upward trajectory is often left totally up to chance. To use an analogy, today's marketing strategies are trying to fill a bottomless pit. New consumers are pushed into the pyramid on one end, only to see them jump ship again halfway up the ladder. This leaves them to move on to the competition long before any profit is made off them.

Let's look at this from the other end of the spectrum: Why should a consumer be persuaded to buy your products with commercials and advertising pressure alone when the following are applicable to them:

- There are a multitude of products out there for every category and an excess of supply.

- The consumer is most likely already using one of these products. Why would anyone switch to something they do not know?

- Buying a new and unknown product always brings risk with it and the possibility of a bad purchase.

To ensure survival and long-term success, brands need heavy users and brand advocates. Something so important should not be left to chance or some intermediary that only has their own interests at heart.

Recap: Recruit, Convert, and Turn into Advocates

In this chapter, we discovered that consumers hold brand success hostage and to win over these consumers' favor, you need to appeal to them not just artificially but on a deeper level.

The brand triad was used to explain the importance of affinity to move from awareness to utilization. We also saw what a healthy brand triad looks like in contrast to an unhealthy one. Media agencies often disagree with this point of view, or they simply don't know how to interpret the situation. They lack the tools to make sense of this insight and the will to change their ways as they can still make enough money with what they are doing now.

I sincerely hope you have realized by now that commercials are not sufficient to create an emotional connection strong enough to ensure repeat patronage just as merely switching channels is not a solution.

The brand loyalty pyramid shows how long-term connections with brand users are essential for the creation of a lucrative ROI. It was also made evident how valuable not only regulars, but heavy users and brand advocates are to a brand, thereby convincing you the importance of having a strategy in place for the following:

- the recruitment of new customers
- their conversion to regulars and heavy users
- turning existing loyal users into brand advocates.

Don't leave this up to chance. Doing so would only increase the gap between awareness and sales uplift. Free your brand's success from this hostage situation by taking control of the customer decision journey! I will tell you what that is exactly and how to do it in the next chapter.

3. The New Consumer Decision Journey

R.I.P. AIDA model!

"We need to stop interrupting what people are interested in and be what people are interested in."

—David Beebe
VP of Global Creative & Content Marketing at Marriott Intl.

"The customer journey doesn't end when they hit the buy button. It doesn't end upon delivery either. Just because a package has been delivered doesn't mean you've completed your work."

—Amit Sharma,
Founder and CEO of Narvar

We Don't Live in an Ideal World

In the last chapters, we determined that in order to make a sale... no, in order to ever be considered by consumers, brands need to create affinity, but not the superficial kind created in brand messages and distributed via mass channels. A deeper emotional connection is needed. This, however, will still not ensure loyalty, and only loyalty will guarantee profit and success. The gap between awareness and sales uplift will not close by itself. And it will not happen organically if you waste the bulk of your budget on the bottom step of the brand loyalty pyramid.

If you want to invest your advertising budget more strategically in a functioning, scalable growth model, you need to take into consideration how consumers make purchasing decisions in the first place. You need to know the who, what, when, and how. Only then can you be present at every crucial stage of the decision-making process.

Countless number of studies and scientific research projects have tried to answer these questions. I don't presume to know the answer to how and why consumers make all the decisions that they make. On the other hand, if we retrace the steps taken during the decision-making process from a consumer's perspective and consider some psychology, it becomes clear that commercials on mass media channels are not the solution but merely a drop in the ocean. In fact, they are more likely to play them into the hands of your competitors—those that have already implemented smart marketing strategies.

When it comes to a consumer's decision-making process, many marketers still refer to the AIDA model, which moves from **A**wareness to **I**nterest, **D**esire, and finally, **A**ction. However, this is an antiquated pattern that has long since been overthrown. If you have not realized this yet, let me explain why this is the case. The AIDA model is obsolete because this model does not only ignore the complexity of modern purchasing decisions but also ignores anything that comes after the initial sale. The entire post-purchase experience is overlooked. No attention is paid to ensuring customer satisfaction, repeat patronage, and advocacy. This kind of model also ignores the crucial feelings of consumers toward the brand and relies too much on a linear response. It is wholly inadequate to represent the buyer journey today, almost dangerously simplistic, and thus, misleading.

Google has this to say on the topic:
"In an ideal world, the journey people take to become loyal customers would be a straight shot down a highway: See your product. Buy your product. Use your product. Repeat.
In reality, this journey is often more like a sightseeing tour with stops, exploration, and discussion along the way—all moments when you need to convince people to pick your brand and stick with it instead of switching to a competitor."

The circular model of the consumer decision journey as introduced by McKinsey is much better equipped to take all these moments into consideration.

A Complex Process:
The New Consumer Decision Journey

If you think back to all the trends discussed in the first chapter, it becomes evident that the consumer decision journey has grown increasingly complex in recent years. Competition has multiplied, and consumers have higher demands. Additionally, with the rise of digitalization, the available marketing channels have increased exponentially. Plus, your customers no longer have to make an uninformed purchase decision as vast amounts of data are available online and offline. People now do research and consult friends about a product before buying it. A circular consumer decision journey predates any purchase today and comprises six phases. A trigger sets in motion the initial consideration, followed by the active evaluation, the moment of purchase, and the post-purchase experience, which, in the best-case scenario, will result in a loyalty loop. We will now look at each of these in turn from different points of view.

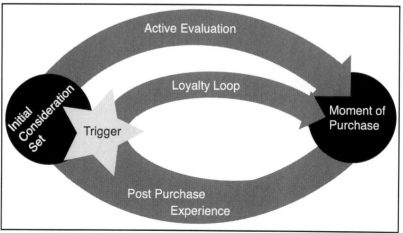

Consumer decision journey (according to McKinsey)

1. The Trigger

This is the first step in every journey—an initial event that brings about a want or need for a product.

Consumer perspective

It could be that you dropped your phone and suddenly need a new one. Or you ran out of milk and desperately want some cereal. Or maybe your coffee maker is getting old and slow. I mean, how could anyone ever expect to get up in the morning without having coffee? Or you might have a hot date scheduled and absolutely need a new scent. Of course, in some instances, a TV commercial may have the potential to be a trigger. Google calls this a micro-moment: an intent-rich moment when a person turns to a device to act on a need—to know, go, do, or buy. They have specified four kinds of micro-moments:

💡 "I want to know" moments
- You are exploring/researching but not necessarily in the purchase mode.
- E.g., you might be going on a diet and start looking for healthy snack choices, or want to find out if it is still possible to redirect an order.

📍 "I want to go" moments
- When someone is looking for a local business or a nearby store.
- E.g., you are on your way to visit relatives and decide to bring flowers. So, you look for a flower shop nearby.

⚡ "I want to do" moments
- When someone wants help to complete a task or try something new
- E.g., you want to make curry and need a recipe and list of ingredients. Or you have a red wine stain on your shirt and need to find out how best to remove it.

⌨ "I want to buy" moments
- When someone is ready to make a purchase but unsure what, where, or how to buy it.
- E.g., you need a new leash for your dog and start comparing prices online.

<u>Brand perspective</u>

The main takeaway here is that, even though advertisements and commercials have the potential to become a trigger, they usually don't. Many marketers sense a chance here and think traditional mass media is the holy grail in this respect. They pressurize the consumers until they attain enlightenment and buy the product. However, all this will result in is annoying the consumer. More often than not, people are triggered by ordinary occurrences in their daily lives. These occurrences precede advertisements and are usually more effective.

2. Initial Consideration Set

This part of the journey is where top-of-mind awareness—the first brands that come to mind when thinking about a product category—comes into play.

<u>Consumer perspective</u>
So, you decide to get a new mobile phone/carton of milk/ coffee maker/perfume. You start thinking about which brands out there sell what you want and need. You may not actively start making a list, but this process happens unconsciously. Previous knowledge and experience are crucial here since you will probably first think about the products you have tried and used before.

<u>Brand perspective</u>
Marketers often believe that with enough advertising pressure, they will achieve top-of-mind awareness and beat out the competition early on in this race for consumers. It is not for nothing that aided and unaided brand awareness reached this level of importance on marketing checklists. —Bollocks!

According to McKinsey, depending on the industry or sector, an average of two brands enter the race at this point. However, just because they were there first, it does not mean they will be victorious in the end.

3. Active Evaluation
The real challenge begins in this phase. This part of the journey is crucial.

Consumer perspective

You start to do some serious research by comparing prices and ingredients. What are the new mobile phones on the market? Is there a bigger container of milk available (so you don't have to go to the store every day)? What is available online and offline? Are there any product ratings available? Can one of your friends recommend something to you? Or could you ask what kind of fragrance your coworker was wearing the other day? It smelled fabulous.

When buying a new coffee maker, you might initially only consider the brand of the one you had. Then, you may start to do some research and find one you have never heard of before. This new coffee maker has more product ratings and several seals of approval. So you start considering and even preferring it over the one you originally favored.

Brand perspective

Marketers usually do not think this far ahead. They are no longer paying any attention to the consumers and leave them to their fate, hoping for the best. By now, these marketing professionals have moved on to the next campaign—the next impression to be generated.

For those that do so, it will be interesting to know that about 88% of consumers do online research before making any purchase on or offline. Some go to the store to try products before buying them, often for a lower price, online, which is called showrooming. Others do online research before purchasing offline (ROPO), which is called webrooming and is practiced by 39% of buyers. 82% of consumers consult their phones before making in-store purchases. Plus, according to Google, a full 70% of Americans now say they look at product reviews before making any purchase. Reviews are increasingly gaining importance. We will get into more detail on this topic in one of the following chapters.

This is where your competition is most likely to swoop in and take over. Again, depending on the sector, another brand or two enter the race here. Your initial ad is most likely no longer being considered by the consumer at this point. Swaying your potential consumer now requires far less money, so you should make sure to be represented at all critical touchpoints, the number of which is steadily increasing. In 2011, the average consumer came across 10.4 touchpoints before making a decision (only 5.3 in 2010). In consumer electronics, there is an average of 14.8 different touchpoints in this phase of the consumer decision journey alone. This means your competitors have 15 different chances to convince your customer to switch sides.

To give you a practical example of what these touchpoints could look like, imagine you want to get an Apple Watch.

There are experience touchpoints:
- You already own an iPhone.
- You use iTunes.
- You use a MacBook at work.

Then there are observational touchpoints:
- A friend already has an Apple Watch.
- You saw it in a James Bond movie.
- Pharrell Williams owns one.
- Steve Jobs' biography is your favorite book.
- There was a story on Apple in the newspaper recently.

Word-of-mouth touchpoints
- Your best friend recommended it to you.
- You read consumers comments on social media.
- You went through the online reviews.

In-store touchpoints
- You have visited the Apple Store.
- You went to a different electronics store that also happens to sell Apple watches.
- You have discussed the watch with a salesperson.

Advertising touchpoints
- You were exposed to advertising.
- You saw promotional material.
- You visited the Apple website/social media pages.

This stage of the journey is also referred to as Zero Moment of Truth (ZMOT), a term coined by Google. No matter what it is we want or buy, the internet has given us the ability to find out everything we want to know. There is no need to blindly grab something and hope for the best anymore. We no longer make any uninformed purchase decisions. Instead, we can look everything up online and then make a decision.

4. Moment of Purchase

This is the First Moment of Truth (FMOT)—the point where the AIDA model and, basically, all classical models end carelessly.

Consumer perspective

Now that you have finally made your decision, you go ahead and buy or order your latest heart's desire. But even now, a salesclerk, an ad, or a discount could sway you.

Brand perspective

For most brands, this part of the journey is out of their control. Retailers make the final decision about positioning on shelves and promotions. Even those marketers who are smart enough to stick around during the active evaluation phase will leave the consumers to themselves after this point. Once the sale is made, their job is done. A lot of money was spent to create awareness, to optimize the point of sale, but then who is to say that next time something comes up, the consumer will make the same choice, come to the same conclusions? If you do nothing else to encourage and affirm your customer, you can only rely on luck. Most brands have no strategy for what happens next.

Linking back to the brand loyalty pyramid, this would be the trial stage. Consumers may have bought/tested your product once. However, unless they are convinced to stay, they are very likely to switch to another brand next time. This is potentially fatal, especially for FMCG products.

5. Post Purchase Experience

Here is where the important part starts, which makes perfect sense if you think about it because the time after the purchase is equivalent to the time before the next one, which depends on whether your consumers had a bad, average, or excellent experience.

Consumer perspective

Here you go, you finally get to take your new acquisition home with you and try it out. Best case scenario, you love it. You brag to your friends about all the crazy features your new phone has or invite them over to have coffee from your new coffee maker. Maybe you'll even give the product a five-star rating on an online review. Worst case scenario, the product is awful. You hate it. You get a rash from the perfume, and the milk has turned sour. The store doesn't want to give you a refund, and nobody reacted to your complaint. Therefore, your next move is to go on social media and tell the world about it.

Brand perspective

This phase actually has several moments of truth which are missed entirely.

There is the Second Moment of Truth (SMOT), referring to the actual use of and experience with the product. Having a great quality product is essential—obviously! Not even the best marketing strategy can convince any consumer to repurchase a product they didn't like. If a consumer is unhappy with the product, there is no way that person will ever buy it again. On top of that, the disgruntled consumer will tell others not to do so either. Bill Bernbach put it this way, "Good advertising kills a bad product faster. It will get more people to know it's bad." He knew what he was talking about even back then.

This brings us to the Third Moment of Truth (TMOT)—the instance when feedback is given to the brand about the product. In this instance, the consumer literally holds your success hostage. Thanks to the technological developments discussed in the first chapter, the consumer can now potentially reach thousands of others. At this point, one consumer becomes the ZMOT for another. So you need to show your customers that you care about them and help them enjoy your product, preferably with personalized communication and after-sales marketing.

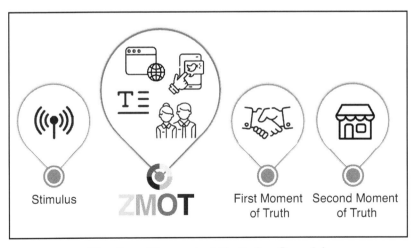

The Zero Moment of Truth (by Google)

There is also the Actual Moment of Truth (AMOT), which is the time between the purchase and the delivery. For your customers, this is a very exciting moment in the journey. Make sure to keep them updated on your progress and use this time of heightened attention to your advantage.

6. Loyalty Loop/Active Re-evaluation

This is not the last step of the journey. Instead, it is the beginning of a new one.

Consumer perspective

You were so happy with this product that the next time you need one of these things, you might just go for the exact same one. Maybe you finally get used to iOS and actually prefer it over Android. Or, and let's be honest here, how often do you really think about which milk to buy? You don't; you just get the same one you always do. Maybe your hot date turned into a success, so you are going to stick with the scent. On top of that, you recommended it to all your friends and family, thereby becoming a brand advocate and a trigger who initiated a new consumer decision journey for someone else.

Thanks to all the developments discussed at the beginning of the book, this is the most crucial step: gaining loyal buyers and users and turning them into advocates. As I mentioned before, in FMCGs, a product will not be successful or profitable if this stage is not reached. This is what all brands should aim for.

Consumer-Centric Marketing

There are some who are still tempted to think that solely focusing on building (top-of-mind) awareness is a sure-fire way to victory in this decision challenge. You might have guessed already that it is not! It may give you a slight advantage at first. If, however, the consumers have insufficient sympathy for your brand, they will immediately dismiss it. Even if there is a high level of sympathy, the research done by consumers in the evaluation stage might expose them to other brands—brands that have strategically invested in marketing along valuable touchpoints.

If you think about it like this, the millions you had invested in advertisements on mass media channels might potentially be the initial trigger to start the consumer decision journey. However, if that is the only thing you do, your competition with more strategic marketing might profit from it. There is too much competition out there to ignore it and too many touchpoints at which they can interfere. You need to help your consumers along their journey. You need to gain their trust. Therefore, it is essential that you shift your focus. Instead of allotting 90% of your marketing budget to mass media channels, you should spread it out cleverly across the entire journey. Invest in your consumers not by giving them a price advantage but by gaining their sympathy, making them loyal, and having them advocate for you.

As Amazon CEO Jeff Bezos has put it, "The most important single thing is to focus obsessively on the customer. Our goal is to be earth's most customer-centric company."

These days, this is true not only for e-commerce companies and retails but increasingly so for brands. Touchpoints need to be filled with content and opportunity for the consumer to find relevant information fast and easily so that they will be convinced about your brand and product.

To meet the "right person" at the "right time" and in the "right place," you should know your target audience and be present when and where they come looking. Give them quick and easy access to the information they want. Most importantly, do not ignore them once you have made the sale. You are responsible for improving their experience and their perception of you.

Recap:
Things Aren't What They Used To Be

To get you started on the consumer decision journey, something happened that makes you want a new product. You initially consider the brands and products you already know and then do some research and actively evaluate them. After that comes the moment you purchase a product, and finally, you decide whether you like it and whether you will consider getting it again.

This chapter showed that we do not live in an ideal world. Things are no longer what they used to be. As seductive as the belief in automatic conversion to loyalty is, it is merely self-deception. Relying on overhauled ideas like the AIDA model will lead you to neglect essential touchpoints along the journey. Instead of only focusing on becoming a trigger and having a high standing in the initial consideration set, you should ensure your presence during active evaluation. If you don't, you will only give an advantage to those that are. Also, you need to enhance the post-purchase experience of your customers, thereby creating a loyalty loop. The time after the purchase is the time before the next purchase. Help your customers convert to brand advocates, and don't leave this crucial aspect of your brand health to chance. You should shift your focus away from first-time users, think further, and start investing in the top of your brand loyalty pyramid. Only then can you close the gap.

4. Brand Loyalty
Customer Retention

"Great companies that build an enduring brand have an emotional relationship with customers that has no barrier. And that emotional relationship is built on the most important characteristic, which is trust."

—*Howard Schultz,*
Chairman Emeritus, Starbucks

"Today, when you're marketing a brand, you can't try to appeal to everybody. You should speak to a group of people and create them as loyalists."

—*Barry Sternlicht,*
CEO of Starwood Capital Group
& Board Member of Estée Lauder Companies

The Unwavering

In Chapter 2, we talked about the brand loyalty pyramid and determined the economic importance of loyal consumers. In Chapter 3, we saw how the customer decision journey could be shortened by enforcing a loyalty loop. In both cases, loyalty enhances value for the brand. Loyalty is clearly vital to brand success. All marketers should realize this; however, some of you might still have questions like these:

- What do you get out of it?
- Why is loyalty ≠ loyalty and what kinds of loyalties are there?
- How do you protect your loyal customers from the competition?
- What is needed to build and retain a base of loyal customers?
- What do consumers really expect from you as a brand?
- What can you do to trigger loyalty? What are the tools to use in the after-sales process?
- How can you measure the success of customer retention strategies?

I'll try to answer all these questions within this chapter, starting with several reasons why exactly it should be one of your main goals to increase and retain a consumer's loyalty towards your brand and its products.

The Brand Perspective

Some of the economic advantages have been mentioned in the previous chapters. For example, a 5% increase in heavy users and brand advocates increases profit by 25% to 100%. This is because loyal customers are far more profitable. They buy more different kinds of products from a brand, they cost less to serve, they buy more often, and they are less price-sensitive than new customers. Also, loyal users, especially advocates, bring in new customers. Loyal customers are happy with your product and want to share it with their peers. They, in turn, are then more likely to become loyal advocates themselves.

Additionally, by reducing the churn of consumers, you save on acquisition costs, which is far more than any retention cost. Plus, there are no acquisition costs for the new customers that your loyals bring into the business. On top of that, it adds to your base profits, which means you get the following benefits:

1. Increased revenue
2. Money is saved
3. Increased sales

So, in comparison to a new consumer, a loyal is much more valuable to you. This will become even more apparent when the two categories are compared side by side.

First-Time Customer

- Promotions sent to new customers have a conversion rate of less than 1%.
- The likelihood of a new customer buying from you is only 5%–20%, and for existing customers, it is 60%–70%.
- Less than 20% of first-time customers will repeat their purchase at full price.
- It costs up to seven times more to acquire a new customer than retain old ones.
- Most businesses need to retain customers for no less than a year, or one and a half, in order to cover acquisition costs.

Loyal Customer

- These customers are worth ten times their first purchase on average.
- 80% of your profits come from 20% of the customers who are loyal.
- A 10% rise in retention can generate a 30% increase in brand value.
- Loyal users ordinarily spend 33% more than new customers.
- Increasing retention by 2% can decrease costs by 10%.

Your individual customer lifetime value is a good indicator of how well your brand is doing. It shows you the worth of your customers. Measuring the profit you make off them throughout their patronage allows you to determine exactly how valuable they are to you.

All these reasons should make it evident that it is only

helpful and profitable for your brand to take steps towards customer retention by taking actions to increase the number of repeat customers and increase the profitability of existing customers. In other words, acquisition creates the foundation of your customer base, but retention is the strategic amplification of relations with consumers and maximization of the revenue each one creates. This also helps to translate awareness into sales. Therefore, you should increasingly shift your focus towards this goal.

Loyalty ≠ Loyalty

You might be wondering what this subtitle is supposed to mean. How could loyalty not be loyalty? Well, it is simple actually. There are four kinds of loyalty or four stages of it. There is spurious loyalty, transactional loyalty, functional loyalty, and emotional loyalty. It is essential for a brand to choose carefully which kind of loyalty to build on. You will see what I mean when we go through them.

1. Spurious Loyalty

As can clearly be determined by the name, this is not real loyalty. This is more of a coincidental circumstance than a conscious decision. Spurious loyalty is most likely based on situational circumstances, such as simple convenience or a lack of alternatives.

From a consumer's point of view, this would look something like this: You always buy the same brand of laundry detergent and have done so for years. However, it has nothing to do with you being particularly fond of the brand or product.

You simply end up buying the same one because the store near your apartment does not have any others.

Marketers need to be very careful with this kind of loyalty since it is not very stable. A consumer in this category might switch to another brand as soon as it becomes available in a nearby store. This clearly is not the kind of loyalty you want to build on.

2. Transactional Loyalty

Consumers are easily attracted by financial incentives and discounts. An example of a transactionally loyal customer would be someone who consistently buys the same shaving gel as they are happy with the price–performance ratio. If, however, there is a sale on another, similar product, the user has no reluctance to switch to something new.

Discounts are an ideal solution to bring in new customers. Removing hurdles and barriers and minimizing the possibility of buyers' regret makes it easier for people to take a chance and switch products. It can build long-term loyalty via initial retention. However, this is not the best kind of loyalty. These consumers are very sensitive to bargains and might choose other brands if those offer better deals. So, to really retain these customers, you need to further develop them. Do not make the same mistake so many other brands make. Do not limit yourself to transactional loyalty. Purchase decisions are not solely based on logic and economic incentives.

Many consumers today expect to be rewarded for their loyalty (71%), but at the same time, there are also a lot of people willing to pay more for the brands they really like (39%). Consumers require additional non-monetary value if you expect them to stay and bear the expense.

3. Functional Loyalty

This kind of loyalty stems from the benefits a consumer gets from being loyal—those that go beyond financial incentives. Some examples could be overnight shipping, premium content, or early access to new product releases. By giving these kinds of opportunities to only a select few of your consumers, you make them feel very special and appreciated. They, in turn, become even more loyal since they get additional value, such as access to certain perks that go beyond price cuts. This kind of loyalty is often associated with brand communities. While this already sounds great, there is still room for improvement. Consumers in this stage of loyalty might still be enticed away by your competition with better offers.

4. Emotional Loyalty

This is the strongest kind of connection you can have with your customers, and the one every brand should be striving to attain. This is the only true kind of loyalty. These emotionally loyal consumers are devoted fans. They will recommend you to others and defend your brand if necessary. This kind of loyalty is not based on receiving any kind of benefit. It does not even have to do with a specific product but, instead, is a deep-rooted relation to the brand and what it stands for.

In other words, emotional loyalty is not a behavioral outcome but a state of mind. These are your brand advocates—your most valuable assets.

The importance of all these kinds of loyalists is the relationship they develop with the brand. The more direct, personal, and deeply rooted the relation, the more loyal they become and the less likely they will be to switch to other brands. It is immensely beneficial to increase the number of loyal consumers your brand has as loyal buyers spend 300% more per year than any new customers do.

What do you think? Which kind of customer would you prefer?

Spurious	Tranactional	Functional	Emotional
Loyalty is based on convenience	Expects some financial benefit	Expects special perks	Unconditional devotion
Whatever, as long as it is close by.	It has to be cheap.	What else can you offer me?	They are the best ever. Period!

What Consumers Expect:
Instill and Retain Loyalty

As you must have surely realized while reading about the kinds of loyalty, a potential customer will not become loyal on their own. There always needs to be a benefit to the consumer. Otherwise, getting them to switch over from the competition or holding on to them is not a simple feat, especially in an oversaturated market like FMCG. Users do not simply fall in love with a brand or product and stick with it for the rest of their lives. They need some sort of incentive from or connection to the brand.

It should be clear by now, how much potential is wasted by merely focusing on customer acquisition, GRP, and reach. You need to build up an emotional relationship with your customers. You need to give your consumers a reason to stick with you. Having a great product is the basis upon which all your success rests, but it is not enough to stay in business.

Consumers today want to have a real, close relationship with their favorite brands. They want to be addressed personally because that makes them feel appreciated. You, as a brand, should really try to get your consumers involved and engaged. Ask for their input and advice. That way, they will feel like they are part of a community. They will trust your brand more and deepen their emotional attachment to you. Consumers should identify with a brand and feel good about supporting their cause.

By instilling loyalty in your consumers, you effectively block the advances of your competition to them. This is partly because, as we know from the customer decision journey, the loyalty loop shortens the journey, and it increases the likelihood that a consumer will choose your brand again.

Trigger Loyalty: Tools

There is a whole array of methods and opportunities you, as a brand, can use to trigger, increase, or retain loyalty. What works best can vary across industries and even from brand to brand. Therefore, it needs to be tested.

1. Improve Customer Service

Good customer support requires clear and effective communication with your consumers. A live chat can be a valuable tool here. It can turn questions into sales and complaints into solutions. Customers can be serviced right away, which only improves their experience. Dealing with complaints quickly and efficiently can easily turn an unhappy customer into a loyal advocate. Such tools enhance personal relations with customers.

Ruffwear is a good example here. They use their live chat in a very creative way. For one thing, their chat agents' profile pictures are icons of dogs. Chats are instigated proactively on specific pages of the website. Thereby, they create a perfect equilibrium between customer self-service and personalized support that is just a click away.

2. Support Charity

It might also be a good idea to support a non-profit cause—show your consumers the values you hold most dear and let them share in it. It is much easier for people to be loyal to beliefs. Being able to provide deeper value, not merely financial, to your consumers gives you the opportunity to connect on a different level and sets you apart from other brands. This point is becoming more important seeing as 53% of consumers believe that it is up to companies, not governments, to create a better future. However, you should be careful to choose a cause that fits with your sector and target audience or you will be accused of greenwashing.

The brand TOMS Shoes, for example, is committed to improving lives. Their famous "One for One" initiative promises to donate a pair of shoes to a child in need for every pair that is purchased from them. Today, they also support clean water initiatives, maternal health care, and organizations like the Wildlife Conservation Society.

3. Show Appreciation

The best way to turn first-time buyers into loyals is to show them how much you appreciate them. Small gestures often go a long way in getting customers to tell the world how great you are, so really get them involved in your strategy. The most important part here is that these gestures are memorable and meaningful, sincere, unexpected, and affordable.

Handwritten note to customers from Casper

What your consumers consider meaningful differs. This is something that can vary across different demographics or even from individual to individual. However, they all will be able to tell if your appreciation is sincere. So, if you don't mean it, don't say it. Also, if you are simply copying what others are doing, there will be no value in it for the consumer. Instead, give them something unexpected while taking care not to overdo it. Even showing appreciation should be financially sustainable.

4. Start a Customer Loyalty Program

This is a great option for online as well as offline purchases. You can introduce a system that allows customers to collect points for every product they buy. They could either be accredited to them directly if they shop online or they could upload a bill from a retail store from where they bought your product. Offering rewards for a certain amount of collected points will incentivize them to buy more often. You could also give the most loyal consumers exclusive benefits.

Here, I need to mention Sephora's Beauty Insider rewards program. It has more than 25 million loyal members, and they are responsible for 80% of their annual sales. These members do not simply get rewards from collecting points, but they can choose how to spend their collected points themselves. The possibilities extend from gift cards to limited edition products and even in-store beauty tutorials. This model allows customers to choose what they really want, which awards additional value to the relationship.

5. Add a Gamification Aspect
Turning a loyalty program into a game adds additional value for the consumers. It makes interacting with your brand more interesting and fun, thereby encouraging repeat customers and even strengthening your brand image. Here, as with anything else, you should not overdo it. For all competitions, the rewards should be achievable., which means you should not offer just one prize to a thousand participants. If you minimize risks for participants, they will not feel cheated.

An illustration of this kind of gamification could be those by Manner, an Austrian confectionery. They regularly launch new products and distribute them among loyal users. They are then asked to upload photos or mention the brand or product on social media. The participants with the most activity and engagement get extra goodies. This way, the brand does not simply strengthen the relation with the customer but also reaches other potential customers via very trustworthy channels.

Manner launch campaign

Measuring Brand Loyalty

There are countless ways to measure the success of your loyalty programs and customer retention efforts. The optimal way to do so differs among companies as it depends on a myriad of variables. However, there are a few metrics that need to be mentioned here as they are most commonly used and always helpful. There are, again, two kinds of metrics: the economic metrics and the involvement metrics.

Economic Metrics

- Customer retention rate (**CRR**): Find out how long the average user sticks with your brand and continually try to increase the number.

- Customer lifetime value (**CLV**): This is the average predicted net profit a customer will bring to your brand during your relationship. You need to keep tabs on variations in this metric. A good and healthy brand should have a steadily increasing CLV.

- Share of wallet (**SoW**): This metric measures how much of your profit stems from loyal repeat customers as opposed to first-time buyers. You should definitely track how this number changes over time.

- Churn rate (**CR**): This is the opposite of CRR. In other words, it is the rate at which users defect from your brand to your competition.

- Negative churn rate (**NCR**): This is what you want to measure: it's not the amount of people that leave but the ones that upgrade and increasing purchases. You want the amount of spending by existing customers to outweigh the amount of revenue lost by exiting customers.

- Net Promoter Score (**NPS**): This is another metric you should be tracking. We already know how valuable promoters are to a brand. How to calculate it and the general advantages of this incredible score will be discussed in detail in the next chapter.

Involvement Metrics

- Engagement: Your content's reach is determined by the number of people that see it, even if only for a moment, which is a vanity metric that means little. Engagement, in contrast, is the number of people that interacted with your content.

- Monthly active users (**MAU**): Merely looking at member count does not really tell you what you want to know. The active members are the interesting ones. The inactive ones can be incorporated in a retargeting campaign.

- Amount of comments (**AoC**): This metric is pretty self-explanatory.

- Share of voice (**SoV**): This metric concerns the amount of advertising and content your brand publishes in comparison to other brands.

All these metrics will help you, as a brand, to determine the success of your loyalty program or customer retention efforts in general. These metrics are much more informative and meaningful than an outdated KPI-like reach could ever be.

The above-mentioned tools to trigger loyalty are just that—tools. If you want to go about instilling and retaining loyalty in a professional manner, you need more than mere selective measures. You need a holistic loyalty strategy, one that fully covers all measures and metrics. The ultimate method to get consumers engaged and retain them in the long term is by creating a brand community. Therefore, this topic deserves some special attention.

Build a Community

The best way to turn your customers into loyals is to build a brand community, a documented personalization strategy. By doing so, you will gain the ability to build trust and emotional connections with consumers—the kind that turns them into loyals.

89% of consumers are loyal to brands that share their values. To know what these values are, you need data. Collecting first-party data will permit you to deliver customized content.

Most FMCG brands do not understand their consumers. They do not even know who these consumers are. They only have a very basic understanding of demographics and purchase history as the information they receive are from third parties. This makes creating personalized content very challenging. Without direct contact, there is also no way to deliver it.

A brand community will make it possible to give community members exclusive experiences and the chance to connect with like-minded consumers. You can then engage in a real two-way conversation and incentivize community members to share content with and about your brand, thereby generating more recommendations. But we will get to that in the next chapter.

An additional major advantage of a brand community is that you have direct access to a forum that is happy to engage with your brand. This means that you can gain some real insight, receive real-time feedback, and test new marketing strategies. Most consumers (four out of five) enjoy giving feedback and are more than happy offer input if it helps a brand they love. Acting on received feedback also has the effect of making consumers even more loyal. Moreover, a community can help save up to 25% in customer support costs annually.

There are two kinds of communities. The open customer community allows access to anyone. This type of community is great for bringing in new members and showing the world how transparent and loved your brand is. Then there are closed or exclusive customer communities. This exclusivity makes the community more appealing and attractive. These are the communities people are willing to pay to get access to.

Case: NIVEA Club

A notable example is the Nivea Club. Every new member receives a gift card or gift sets of their choice worth 15€. They get the chance to try new products and receive a 10% discount in the online shop. There are additional benefits for referring friends and much more. Members even receive a little gift for their birthday. Before you turn away thinking this can't possibly bring any profit, let me tell you that people actually pay an annual fee to become members of this exclusive club.

Little gifts make them feel appreciated. In addition to that, they become part of a real brand community. For the brand, this has the advantage of getting direct access to their most loyal fans and a panel to try new products and marketing strategies on. This panel or community will, in turn, give the brand valuable input and feedback on their products. Advocates can be deliberately activated to create tons of recommendations and other content on and offline.

Nivea club website (club.nivea.at)

4 Problems within Corporations

During one of my business trips, I met a very interesting woman. She was the brand community manager of one of the few international brands that have an active community. We both agreed on the incredible benefits any brand would reap if they started a community. She said that 80% of the brand's revenue stems from her club members. I asked her why there are still so many brands without one, why traditional brands and big conglomerates don't seem to notice the opportunity they are missing out on, and why they treat customer retention and loyalty with such blatant disregard.

Here is What She Told Me:
There are four major problems within corporations.

1. Translation problems: Goals are mistranslated from one team to the next, leading them to aim for moronic goals.

For example, if a CEO wants to increase margins or revenue, this is translated into a different KPI for the marketing department. Here, higher revenue suddenly means increasing reach and ad pressure and creating higher awareness.

However, by considering the brand loyalty pyramid, we know by now that these goals are not in line with real brand success. To increase revenue, the existing user base should be further developed from regulars to heavy users and advocates, which will turn loyalty into a much more useful KPI for management to realize.

2. Maturation problems: Marketing goals are becoming stagnant. They don't build on one another. Instead, marketers always fall back to zero as if nothing ever happened.

Instead of starting with the recruitment of new brand users and moving on to the development of these users into loyals and advocates, brands keep on starting anew. This means that every year, they focus on promoting awareness again instead of trying to convert that awareness into something more. Every year, they fill the bucket with fresh water and don't care how much leaks out of the holes in the bottom.

3. Horizontal cooperation problems: The left hand does not know what the right is up to. Everyone is (moronically) aiming for their personal goals without realizing that their resources could be pooled to achieve multiple goals simultaneously.

For example, one individual may be trying to acquire as many new newsletter subscribers as possible, but the quality of these subscribers is irrelevant. To this person, it does not matter if these subscribers could help fulfill other goals within the organization. Another person is expected to generate sales and they allocate their entire budget for a completely different channel. They don't join forces or funds. Even though their individual KPIs are high, there is not much worth in them. However, if they combined their efforts, they could generate high-quality leads—leads that fit the target audience, increase the subscribers to the newsletter, and then convert into users.

The results might come in a smaller volume with fewer subscribers and less awareness. They would, however, have a clear funnel in place to onboard new customers.

4. Vertical cooperation problems: The same issue also applied for cross-selling.

One person may be responsible for a deodorant and another for a shampoo of the same brand. There is no coordination or cooperation between the two. Instead, both have their own budgets invested in awareness, one for the shampoo and the other for the deodorant.

This is the example she gave me: If the CEO wants to increase margins, this goal is generally used to dispose of seemingly pointless expenses.

Often, this includes CRM efforts. Investing in existing customers is (illogically) not seen as cost-effective, especially when they could instead be investing in new customers by promoting awareness. Additionally, expenses like packaging, content changes and internal budget cuts are tinkered with. The fact that it would be sensible, in the long term, to focus on loyalty and establish a community—one that could cost-effectively be used for cross- and up-selling-promotions—is never even considered.

Admittedly, it would be a little late to introduce this method if the goal is set on increasing margins, but it would be a smart and, in the long run, profitable strategy to start laying the groundwork. Aside from that, it is important to realize that these four problems are not a valid excuse. The market does not care about the internal problems of corporations. Consumers will stop considering your brand as soon as they find a different brand that better serves their needs or if they find a brand they can identify with on a deeper level. These alternatives are already out there, waiting to snatch away your consumers and never let them go again.

Recap: Questions Answered

In this chapter, we discussed the importance of loyal repeat customers and answered some specific questions on the topic.

- We saw that loyalty ≠ loyalty. There are different kinds of loyalty, which are stages that build upon one another. The stronger the relationship between consumers and the brand, the more loyal they are.
- Those that have a deep-rooted emotional loyalty are immune to advances from other brands. They are very unlikely to switch brands.
- The precondition for such a base of loyal customers is sympathy and, thus, consumer insights are required.
- Appreciation, inclusion, community building, etc., are needed because these are things the consumers want and expect from their favorite brands.
- To trigger loyalty, you should give your consumers added value by showing appreciation, supporting charity, starting a loyalty program, adding gamification features, and best of all, by building a community.

- Plenty of performance metrics exist that are more useful than outdated KPIs like reach.
- A few problems must be solved internally: translation, maturation, and cooperation.

Many advantages were described, and loyals were compared to first-time customers.

What you need to take away from this chapter is that loyal users and advocates are infinitely more valuable to your brand than first-time buyers. They are the backbone of any successful brand. Therefore, these loyals deserve much more attention than they are getting today. The focus of brands needs to shift towards consumer centrism and retention. Only then can the gap between awareness and sales uplift be closed.

On a different note, loyalty has an additional benefit. There is one more step by which loyalty can be improved upon. In the next chapter, we will look at recommendations and advocates. They are the best strategy to close the gap between awareness and sales uplift.

5.
Recommendations

Economic advantages

from an unlikely source

"A brand is no longer what we tell the consumer it is—it is what consumers tell each other it is."

—*Scott Cook*
Co-founder of Intuit, Director of eBay and Procter & Gamble

"People share, read, and generally engage more with any type of content when it's surfaced through friends and people they know and trust."

—*Malorie Lucich*
Head of Product Communication of Pinterest

"Courteous treatment will make a customer a walking advertisement."

—*James Cash Penney*
Founder of J.C. Penny

This Comes Highly Recommended

In the previous chapter, loyalty was discussed in detail. This chapter will focus on a specific result loyalty brings about. Brand advocates are located at the highest point of the loyalty pyramid, which means that they are the most loyal customers who will recommend your product and brand to others and can most efficiently help to close the gap. So what does loyalty look like in action? To answer that question, we need to take a consumer's perspective on loyalty.

The concept of loyalty is very value laden. When asked directly, people will not readily associate it with brands. It is much more often attributed to family or country. In other words, you don't think of yourself as being loyal to a brand, you think of yourself as being loyal to your family and friends. So, if you find something you are particularly happy about, a product you really like and the brand behind it, you will tell them about it. Ergo, if consumers are very happy about a new product or brand in general, they might not consciously think about being loyal to the brand. They will, however, recommend it to their friends and family, those that they are loyal to.

The brand loyalty pyramid has already showed the importance of brand advocates and their recommendations. They have incredible economic value and are five times as valuable to your brand as any regular consumer. In spite of that, we have not yet discussed what this actually means: What are recommendations?

There are several definitions out there; however, I interpret the term to mean the following:

"Recommendations, or word of mouth, are all the interactions between two consumers and all the content by consumers that are passed on online or offline."

Recommendations are one of the most effective forms of advertising in marketing. Word of mouth was, in fact, the original form of marketing. Recommendations have been our main source of inspiration since the dawn of humanity, and our entire way of life might actually be based on them. We wouldn't be where we are today without recommendations. Knowledge used to be passed on solely by word of mouth. How to start a fire, how to build tools, our religions, everything we know today was passed on from one person to the next. Throughout history, people gave others information on where the closest market place is, who makes the best bread, and who has the freshest fish.

Over the course of time, the benefits and power of recommendations have been forgotten, and its importance has been denied. However, it is now, just as it was then, the best way to gain new users and the most important propellant in the customer decision journey. Recommendations are the main reason we buy the things we do today.

Let's Talk About Bad Profit

Don't get me wrong here. I'm not saying that profit is bad but that there is bad profit. How can it hurt your business? Focusing on the wrong kind of profit can actually constrict growth. It is bad for your reputation and antagonizes consumers. To put it simply, any profit that is made off unhappy customers is bad. These customers will not only buy less, but they will also promptly defect to the competition and tell anybody who will listen about their unpleasant experience, thus causing others to avoid the brand and product as well. This might not have been too big a problem in the past since there was less competition to switch to and people could probably tell no more than ten others. Today, however, with an ever-increasing number of competitors available and access to the internet, bad publicity can have detrimental consequences for a brand.

Remember that you do not want to prosper at the expense of your consumers. To retain them, you need to ensure that they are happy. Otherwise, they will defect. Earnings should come from customers' passionate participation.

Let me give you an example here which you have probably heard of before. Dell Computers did not always have the best customer service. People were kept on hold for hours, and the fault was always somewhere else; so they were reverted to another person and kept on hold again. One very unhappy customer started a blog about his painstaking experience and called it Dell Hell. This was back in the early days of the internet, but the blog post went viral until, eventually, the New York Times picked up on it. This did considerable damage to the company and its brand reputation. Its stock lost 25% of its value that year.

Quality is of much more worth than quantity. The number of people reached is less important than the experience these individuals had with your brand and product. It is more important that the people you convinced stick with you and recommend your brand to others since first-time users are not yet profitable. This will help you to acquire further happy customers and turn them into advocates.

Loyal brand users are much more valuable to your brand as they provide good profit. They will purchase more frequently than other customers and are interested in a wider range of products. They also provide valuable insight and feedback, are less price-sensitive, and cost less to serve. Most importantly, they will recommend your brand to their friends and become promoters (advocates).

This has obvious benefits. We already know that a 5% increase in retention will result in an increase in profit by 25% to 100%. Also, customers who come to your brand because it was referred to them are more likely to become loyal brand advocates themselves. In addition to that, it is cheaper to retain customers than to acquire new ones. Loyal customers might only amount to an average of 20% of your customer base, but they are responsible for 80% of all sales. Acquiring new customers can be up to 25% more expensive than retaining current ones.

So you see, in order to retain customers, you need to shift your focus away from a profit-centric one to a more customer-centric one. To find out whether your profits are good, you need to track your NPS.

Net Promoter Score (NPS)

Recommendations are essential for you and your brand. They are at the top of your brand loyalty pyramid, and they have a huge impact on your entire company's success.

This makes recommendations an interesting KPI and one that can be put in numbers with the NPS. It helps you measure your consumers' willingness to recommend your brand and product to others. In fact, research across various industries has proven this score significantly correlates with brand success. This can be accredited to the fact that recommendations play a significant role in driving your business performance.

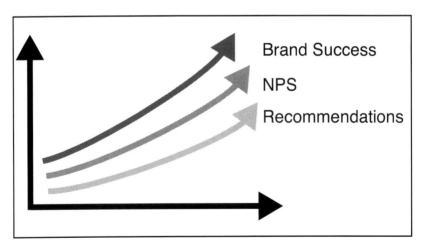

Correlation success, NPS, and recommendations

The score was first introduced by Fred Reichheld in 2003. First things first—it is not simply another measure for customer satisfaction. It is, instead, a key figure that shows the loyalty of customers. However, it is also much more than that. "NPS, ultimately, is a business philosophy, a system of operational practices, and a leadership commitment [...]." It is a shift away from profit-centric orientation towards the customer-centric orientation.

Many Fortune 500 companies, such as P&G, GE, Apple, and Phillips, are using the NPS for reference and advancement. They have realized its worth and that recommendations are no longer uncontrollable natural occurrences. These companies are actively stimulating recommendations and word of mouth because they know NPS leaders profit from a four-time higher industry growth rate compared with brands that have low scores. They also have considerably fewer expenditures when it comes to customer acquisition because their consumers do most of the work for them—for free!

Measuring NPS

The clear advantage of this score is that it not just correlates with brand success, but it is also very easy to obtain. Therefore, it is perfect for evaluating the current situation of your enterprise. All you need to do to calculate it is ask your customers how likely they are to recommend your product, on a scale from 0 (not at all) to 10 (absolutely every time). Based on that, divide the respondents into three clusters. The "detractors" are those who chose options 0 to 6. These consumers will not recommend your product to anyone.

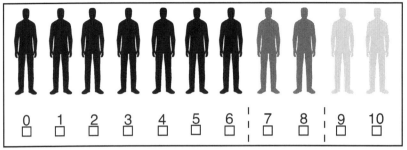

NPS—Promoters, passives, and detractors

The "passives" are the ones who are neutral toward your product and chose option 7 or 8. Finally, the "promoters" are those who chose numbers 9 and 10. These are the only ones who would potentially recommend your product. Now, all you need to do is subtract the percentage of detractors from the promoters, and you'll get the Net Promoter Score.

Recommendations lead to more users, engagement, brand popularity, and ultimately, the growth of your business.

It used to be difficult to measure the precise return from word of mouth, or recommendations. This was a big obstacle for marketers who were trying to embrace it. Today, thanks to McKinsey, we know word of mouth drives an average of 20% to 50% of sales across categories.

I mentioned that Apple uses NPS, but we should take a closer look at how that worked out for them. When they had started out, they had high-quality products but no retail presence. They thus started opening their own stores, partly to revitalize customer service and offer support in the "Genius Bar." This move helped to boost the brand's NPS from 57 to 71 since 2007. Store performance is tracked using the NPS. Any dissatisfied customers are called by the store manager personally and turned from a detractor into a promoter, which means these customers would bring in extra sales of as much as $1000 within a year.

Troublesome Question

There is a problem though which you might have guessed by now. To calculate the NPS for your product, you need to ask the question—"the ultimate question" as Reichheld calls it. To do that, you need direct contact with the actual users of the products. This is not something you can leave to intermediaries like retailers or e-commerce partners. To make full use of the NPS, you need to collect the data first-hand and in real-time. Only then can you use it efficiently. Last week's NPS might be totally different from today's. Only by collecting the data first-hand can you divide it by region or other criteria, which will make it much easier to identify the source of potential problems.

On top of that, merely about 10% of your brand's promoters are indeed active. The other 90% need to be mobilized. This is a huge source of unused potential. These are the consumers that are really valuable to your brand, as you already know, because brand advocates do not simply spend more than an average consumer but also bring in an average of three new users; they are about five times as profitable to a brand.

It is not merely the number of advocates and their recommendations that are of importance to your brand; another aspect to consider is the speed at which they do so.

About two thirds of recommendations still happen offline. They have a direct and indirect impact on your business performance. The impact of one word of mouth impression is equivalent to at least five impressions on paid media. Also, it has a more immediate impact than traditional media, especially in the first two weeks (90% online and 73% offline).

So, once you know if your customers are willing to recommend you, it would also be helpful to know how long it would take them to do so—the faster, the better! This brings us to another very interesting figure, the viral cycle time.

Viral Cycle Time (VCT)

This figure describes the time needed for a consumer to recommend your brand or product to someone else, invite a friend, or share content. It may be counterintuitive, but you want this number to be as low as possible.

For example, you just bought a new sports bottle. You love it, it fits perfectly into the bottle holder on your bike, and the top unscrews into a cup. Two weeks later, you go on a biking trip with friends over the weekend and brag about your new acquisition, maybe even include it in your social media post. In this case, the viral cycle time would be two weeks.

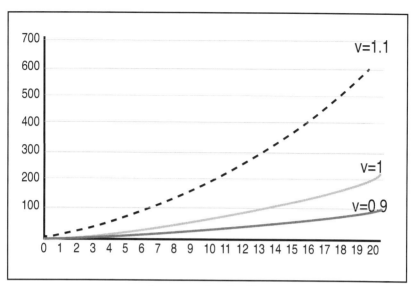

Increase in virality

The lower this number is, the faster people recommend your product to others. Reducing the viral cycle time has the greatest effect on the viral growth of your product. As David Skok, General Partner at Matrix Partners, put it,

"[If during every cycle a user invites two additional users] after 20 days with a cycle time of two days, you will have 20,470 users. But if you halved that cycle time to one day, you would have over 20 million users!"

Therefore, you want to make it as easy as possible for your consumers to find and share information about you. Happy users will automatically want to share their experiences with their friends and family. More shares mean more new users.

This makes recommendations especially useful during the launch of a new product. To explain this, an example would be helpful. So, imagine you just launched a new product. A lot of advertising has been done for it, and many people have already seen it. Valuable time is lost during the launch and barely any profit is being made from the product sales. Why? Your ads and TV commercials might be able to make people curious, but that is not enough to make them want to buy the product. They might still be skeptical. Only once there are enough people who have tried the product, you can observe a steep rise in profit. This is because only recommendations give people the necessary confidence to switch products and try new things. Recommendations help you gain market shares faster, penetrate new markets faster, and achieve quicker success with new products. One way of speeding up this process is by speeding up your VCT.

Basis for Recommendation Success

We have already talked about recommendations extensively, but there is still one question that needs answering: Why do they work so well?

People don't trust commercials anymore or any kind of information originating from brand-owned sources. But we do trust our friends and the recommendations they make. They are also, in contrast to advertisements, much more likely to have our full attention. Plus, they recommend things that are of actual interest and relevance to us. All in all, their recommendations are far superior to anything a brand could do or say because of the following features:

1. Authenticity

What makes these recommendations so effective in comparison to other forms of advertisement is their authenticity. This also has to do with trust. We trust that a friend will recommend a brand or product because they care for us and don't have any ulterior motive. This kind of recommendation will be formulated in their own words and without the cliche-ridden phrases used in advertisements. The words chosen in such a situation are selected unconsciously and aimed at and customized for a specific person, which results in a level of authenticity that is impossible to reach for traditional advertisements. If recommendations are bought and paid for, they lose this altruistic aspect and, thereby, their authenticity.

You might have guessed by now that influencer marketing is not authentic either. People don't attribute the same level of trust to it. An influencer is paid or receives some kind of incentive to advertise and publicly support a brand or product. So, we can't be sure if they actually like and believe in the product. Plus, they most certainly do not recommend it with our best interests at heart.

Only about 18% of people will buy a product that an influencer has recommended. On the other hand, 57% of people under 40 will buy a product because an acquaintance has recommended it on social media. Or to put it differently, only about 10% of people consider recommendations by influencers when buying a product. Further, 42% of people in Germany believe that influencers do nothing but advertise.

2. Push vs Pull

An additional major difference between recommendations and traditional advertisements is that they follow opposing principles. While advertisements are pushed onto people even though they often don't want it, recommendations are usually pulled in by people. For example, if you need a new computer and are not too well versed in this field, you might ask a friend working in IT for advice on what to get. By doing so, you get exactly the information you need and a product tailored to your specific requirements. Thus, you save time and money and avoid the frustration of making a wrong purchase decision. On the other hand, if you look up computers online, you will be bombarded with ads on computers and accessories for weeks to come. Also, the recommendations made by friends will stay with you. You will remember them while you will forget advertisements the second they are gone, if you even realized they were there in the first place.

3. Trust Transfer

Last, but not least, trust transfer needs to be discussed. By definition, trust means taking a risk based on the belief that the other person will act in one's best interest.

In terms of recommendations, this means that the trust one person has in a product or brand is transferred to the next. You believe your friends will recommend a product or brand to you because they are very happy with it and think there is real value in its price, quality, and functionality. Because we trust our friends, we also trust that their recommendations are made in our best interests. Therefore, we also trust the product that is recommended and are more likely to buy it.

On top of that, the people who come in contact with your brand and product are more likely to become advocates themselves.

There is one more difference between recommendations and commercials that we need to address—reach. Obviously, a traditional advertisement will potentially have a much higher reach than a recommendation between two people. A recommendation, however, usually doesn't stay between just two people. There is a 75% chance that people who receive a recommendation will pass it on. If you have thousands of advocates for a product and consider the fact that recommendations are more valuable and effective, the discrepancy is more than made up for, especially if your viral cycle time is low.

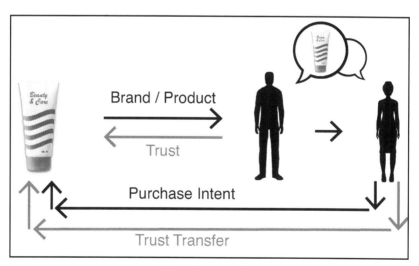

Trust transfer

From what we have heard so far, it seems that pressure is constantly rising. How can you make sure you have your customers' sympathy and trust? How can you make sure you will reach the right person at the right time and palace and with the right message? How can you increase conversion and create brand advocates? The answer is shockingly simple. There is one solution to all these problems—word of mouth advocacy!

Recap: Trusted and Remembered

In this chapter, a new focal point for brands was introduced—the Net Promoter Score and how it can help companies align their goals more towards consumers than towards profit and towards loyalty instead of retention. Sustainable growth is not possible today without it.

Recommendations or word of mouth are the easiest way to gain consumers' trust and build a lasting relationship since both are transferred from one friend to the next. People have relied on recommendations since the dawn of time, but somewhere along the way, marketers have forgotten about them in spite of the extraordinary economic advantage these recommendations bring with them.

The biggest selling point of recommendations with consumers is their authenticity, which is impossible to replicate with commercials. Also, recommendations are not forced on to the consumers when they don't need or want any. Instead, consumers pull recommendations in at exactly the right moment.

The benefits brands gain through customer recommendations are measurable with the Net Promoter Score, which has a direct correlation with the brand's success. By shortening the viral cycle time of a product, these benefits can increase exponentially. In order to get credible intel in a timely manner, you need to collect the data first-hand and not leave it to third parties to do so for you.

Increasing the number of brand advocates you have and having them recommend your product to all their friends and family is crucial. That is the best marketing strategy you could adopt. WOM easily piques a person's interest and even gets others involved in talking about the brand and product. A recommendation by a friend or acquaintance is considered throughout the entire decision journey because it is aimed at the right person, at the right time and place, and with the right message.

WOM is superior to commercials and advertisements as it is the most convincing way to start and influence the active evaluation phase of others. It most efficiently bridges the gap between awareness and sales uplift. We do not trust commercials, but we trust our friends and peers, which includes online user-generated content (UGC). The next chapter will go into more detail about the digital developments that enable us to use UGC and how much untapped potential it has.

x. Influencer (Marketing)

Successful digital strategy or worst naming of the century

"People influence people. Nothing influences people more than a recommendation from a trusted friend. A trusted referral influences people more than the best broadcast message. A trusted referral is the Holy Grail of advertising."
—Mark Zuckerberg
CEO of Facebook

"Successful social media marketing is not built on impressions. It's built on relationships."
—Kim Garst
CEO at KG Enterprises

"Influence is NOT popularity!"
—Brian Solis
Global Keynote Speaker, Digital Analyst and Anthropologist, Strategic Advisor

First Things First

Before we get started with this chapter, let me make one thing clear: I was not planning to write about influencers in this book. There are already countless interesting reads and articles about this topic out there. However, the hype around influencer marketing is continuing and more marketers are blindly following the trend. Therefore, I want to equip you with an alternate perspective on the topic.

The line between the activation of consumers through user-generated content and influencer marketing is fluid? In this chapter, I will make the difference between these things evident.

Since I was not originally planning to write this chapter I decided to turn it into a bonus chapter that you can access for free on our online bonus material: https://www.d2cgrowthrevolution.com/resources#bonus-chapter-influencer

6. How Brands Fail to Digitize

Make better use of the options available to you

"The internet has turned what used to be a controlled, one-way message into a real-time dialogue with millions."

—Danielle Sacks
Senior Editor at Inc. Magazine

"Marketing without data is like driving with your eyes closed."

—Dan Zarrella
Former Social Media Scientist at HubSpot

Traditional vs. Digital-First Brands

As of late, digital advertising has become increasingly caught up in the crossfires of discussion. Demands for transparency and brand safety are growing more adamant. Unilever threatened to cut its digital ad spending drastically while P&G actually did without resulting in any loss of sales and revenue. This leads one to believe that digital marketing does not pay off. At least, it did not for P&G. On the other hand, digital-first brands like Dollarshaveclub.com and Tail.com grow almost exclusively via digital channels.

For those of you who don't know these companies, here's something about them:

Dollar shave club is a subscription service for razor blades. In a market dominated up to 60% by Gillette, this brand sells razor blades at a fraction of the price they cost in retail and sends them directly to the customers' home. Within just 5 short years, the company was sold for $1 billion to Unilever. All of this was done with a digitally focused marketing strategy and without ever opening a physical store.

Tails.com is a subscription service as well for dog food. However, they are taking it a step further with curated shopping. By answering a few short questions, consumers can get the food personalized and individualized for their specific dog. With this ingenious system, the brand grew to ten times its original size within just 3 years. It was then sold to Nestlé for an undisclosed sum.

How could this be? Why does digital advertising work for some but not for others? Is it because of the business model? Is it because of the products? Are long-established brands simply using digital options the wrong way? Have they not yet fully grasped the core of digitization? Or is it merely that companies like Tails.com have their finger on the pulse of time?

These are the questions I will answer in this chapter.

Blurring Lines

Technologies are constantly developing and being refined. All of this is happening in such a rapid and versatile manner that we barely notice it anymore. One thing that should not pass us by unnoticed, however, is that the on- and offline worlds are steadily moving closer together. Thanks to all kinds of new high-tech and software solutions, almost everything has been digitized. Our lives and brands have moved online. We have social media, augmented reality, digital twins, etc. On the other hand, the internet is moving offline. Here, I mean the Internet of things, Amazon Dash Buttons and the like. We now have the 'cloud' and 'big data'. The lines between both worlds are blurring more. The internet, especially Web 2.0, and the development of smartphones have given rise to a myriad of possibilities.

What does this mean for brands in the 21st century?

To think that digitization only refers to communication would be a delusion. However, we will, of course, focus on the impact digitization had on brands in terms of communication, use of data, and especially the relationship between brands and consumers, which explores customer-centricity, automation, and personalization.

Digital Communication

Looking at the current status quo of traditional brands' communication, it becomes clear that the failure to digitize starts here. The divide between both worlds, on- and offline, is still enormous in this respect. It is insufficient in this day and age to simply synchronize brand communication in digital and classical media.

What I mean to say is this: In the past century, brands have become experts in one-way communication. Traditional media didn't allow anything else. Even the internet was a one-way channel in its early days, and website operators used it to distribute information online.

The internet has come a long way since then. It is no longer just about the distribution of information by website operators but the inclusion of users. Simple sender and receiver relationships evolved and brought about the possibility of two-way communication. There was a switch from a one-way road to a platform that enables discussion. This enabled brands to have a more intimate relationship with their consumers.

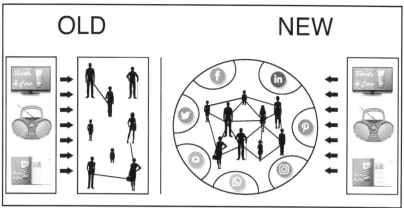

Old vs new model of communication
(according to Digital Patang)

This hidden treasure is still looked upon with fear and suspicion. The inclusion of and communication with consumers do not fit into brands' suffocating straitjacket of classical media planning. Therefore, valuable Web 2.0 channels degenerate into boring and sparsely interactive notice boards. The communication engaged in by most brands is more comparable to a dull monolog than a worthwhile dialog.

It would be a mistake to believe that digital media can be used in the same way as classical media. It is not meant merely for mass-communication. Most brands, however, do not seem to notice this.

Let me give you an example of how to successfully implement a shareable online campaign.

Volvo used the 2015 Super Bowl to their advantage. Super Bowl day is the most expensive advertising day of the year in the United States. Car companies like Fiat, Toyota, and Kia each had spent $4.5M on a 30-second Super Bowl commercial during the Super Bowl that year, while Volvo had only used a fraction of that budget. Instead of airing their own commercial, they hijacked all the other car commercials.

Before the Super Bowl, they spread the word that people could win a Volvo for someone they care about. All they had to do was share the hashtag #VolvoContest and the name of the person they wanted to give it to every time they saw a commercial during the game.

So instead of paying attention to the ads on TV, people were tweeting. The social conversation shifted completely and up to 2,000 #VolvoContest tweets per minute were sent anytime a car commercial aired. Over 55,000 tweets were sent in total.

While the other car brands got their 30-second spots, Volvo got top of mind awareness for days to come.

If you want to know more about the Volvo Interception, check out the online bonus material: https://www.d2cgrowthrevolution.com/resources #volvo-interception

The Volvo example shows that consumers are more interconnected than ever. They have become small media powerhouses. Communication between consumers used to be restricted to their own personal surroundings. Today, they can share their experiences and criticism with the entire world. At the same time, information and the range of products and brands available have never been greater. In this environment, competing brands are always just a click away.

Consumer Channels

Digitalization has had huge influences on recommendations and word of mouth. These have moved online as eWoM or, as I like to call it, consumer channels. This includes any statement made on the internet by potential, actual, or former customers about a product or company.

However, as Slack's CEO Stewart Butterfield has put it,

> *"...even the best slogans, ads, landing pages, PR campaigns, etc., will fall down if they are not supported by the experience people have when they [...] first begin using the product and when they start using it day in, day out."*

You cannot control the kind of content your customers generate. So, I can understand any hesitation you might have about using and even encouraging it. Still, you should know that the positive aspects of UGC far outweigh any potential downside.

UGC triggers a very different response from its audience than content created by professionals, the extent of which you might not yet fully realize. For one thing, UGC is five times more likely to lead to a sale than professional content. In fact, in 2019, 79% of users said that UGC influenced their buying decisions. This has to do with the authenticity accredited to this kind of content. User-generated recommendations and content in the form of reviews, images, and videos appear more trustworthy to consumers than classical brand communication.

A great example of the ideal use of UGC is the #MakeItCount campaign by Nike. Two YouTubers, Casey Neistat and Max Joseph, promoted the hashtag in a travel video. The video went viral and millions of consumers used the hashtag on their own posts. Nike saw an 18% increase in profit that year.

This brings us back to our favorite issue—consumers trust other consumers. Since UGC does not fit into our mental adblocker, we notice it more readily and are more likely to engage with it. You can basically think of UGC as an online recommendation. Actually, 74% of respondents in a study by Olapic stated that they have posted a picture with a brand hashtag before. 40% of them said that the main reason for doing so was to share purchases with their friends. Consumers actively look for this kind of content. Most consumers expect to find it on the brand's website (40%), but 29% will switch directly to Amazon.

Remember the Volvo example? Their stunt resulted in 200 million USD in earned media impressions, and their XC60 model saw a 70% sales increase in the month following the Super Bowl. It's no wonder—thousands of people had effectively recommended the car to people they cared for.

The number of touchpoints at which people search and find information on a brand or product is increasing. Product reviews are becoming especially more relevant. 84 % of people trust online reviews as much as recommendations made by close, personal friends. Especially in the consumer electronics industry, reviews are increasingly important. 97% of people read online reviews before buying any kind of electronics. 62% read five or more reviews.

Even negative comments can be very helpful to your brand as actively engaging with customer complaints can turn a disgruntled customer into your biggest fan. After all, these customers care enough to give you feedback. 91% of consumers will not tell you what made them unhappy and will simply leave. The ones that do give you feedback want you to improve. You should not ignore them; instead, use their input. Studies also show that 45% of consumers are more likely to go to and buy from companies that respond to negative reviews rather than avoid it. Plus, reviews are becoming more positive in general. Since 2010, the level of positivity in online reviews has increased by 12%. On top of that, a few negative reviews boost authenticity. If there are only good reviews for a product, consumers will get suspicious. The ideal rating is between 4.2 and 4.5 stars. With higher ratings, you risk falling into a "too good to be true" category.

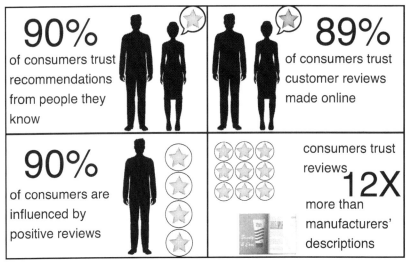

Who do consumers trust? (according to InnovaBiz)

According to a study by Stackla, 90% of people set great store by UGC. 51% of consumers think that less than half of the content created by brands is authentic, while 92% of marketers think that the content they produce is perceived as authentic. So, even though you might think of your content as authentic, this is not necessarily how your customers see it.

While technically influencer content could be defined as user-generated, it is not as authentic. Real UGC by regular people is 9.8 times more likely to impact purchasing decisions than content by influencers. We have already talked about this in detail in the chapter about influencers.

You might now be inclined to think that UGC only works online. However, the blurring between the two worlds becomes evident again with this topic.

Consumers not only search for UGC and reviews when shopping online but also when planning to make an in-store purchase. This phenomenon is known as ROPO (research online–purchase offline) or showrooming, the opposite of which would be webrooming, which is when people get their information in personal sales pitches in-store but then make a purchase online, usually at a discount.

If you let all this sink in, you will realize the importance consumer channels hold for brands. Nonetheless, they are still utterly underrepresented in marketing and media strategies. Maybe this is because brands lack the know-how to use these channels. Maybe it is because the strategies have simply not been designed to use them and it is easier to continue using established methods in a digital domain. Digitization has, after all, also created countless new possibilities in terms of one-to-many communication. Aside from new channels like influencer marketing, email marketing, SEO, and paid social, programmatic advertising has gained a lot of popularity.

The increasing automation in marketing especially seems to be developing into a strong trend for the future.

Automation
By automation, I am not referring to programmatic advertising. While it is a kind of automation, it is not the kind you would most benefit from.

Programmatic advertising is the automated sale of advertising space in real-time. It is very efficient, works in real-time, and can focus on a narrow target group. However, because there is no direct interaction between the seller and buyer, there is high potential for fraud ranging from paying for advertising to bots to the ad simply ending up being obstructed and invisible to its audience. Ads might also end up being redirected and re-brokered and may never even reach the intended audience. On top of that, focusing on narrow target groups is expensive.

The kind of automation that you need is the kind that brings you closer to your consumers. Programmatic advertising is just another way of handing over the reins to someone else. Instead, you should invest in things like chatbots or virtual assistants, such as Alexa and Siri. There are FMCG brands out there already using this kind of tool—Coca Cola, for example. These tools will help you to optimize your customer service and ultimately save money.

The basis for the success of this automation trend in marketing is the collection of data.

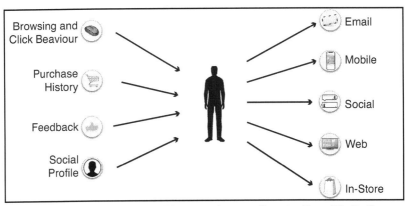

Using consumer intelligence (according to Deg Digital)

Advantages of Data

The new connection between a brand and its consumers makes it possible to create and collect vast amounts of data. It is not the volume I am interested in right now but its value. To be of real value, data should be collected first-hand from the source and in real-time. With digitization, it is no longer necessary to rely on intermediaries to produce incomplete datasets. These are often obsolete by the time you receive them. Let me put it this way: It is much more interesting to know that customer X bought something from you for the third time this month and spent twice as much as he usually does than knowing that product Y has been sold ten times last month.

What you need is real consumer intelligence. To get ahead of your competition, you need to really understand your customers and their needs and wants and fulfill them better than anyone else. In order to do this, you need data and lots of it. You also need the means to gather and interpret the data for valuable insights and consumer trends. To receive the valuable data needed first-hand and get the opportunity to use it to your advantage, you should stop relying on intermediaries such as retailers or agencies to provide it for you.

Unfortunately, many brands are still flying blind today. They have no data to support and inform their decisions. They have no basis to build on. As it was just mentioned, the data they do use is collected by others and is usually purely descriptive. This might work out if your products and sales are going well.

If they are not, you have a problem and no way of identifying its origin. Why is this product not selling? What do people not like about it? Is it simply not what they are looking for right now? There are countless reasons a product may not sell, but without asking the consumers, you will never know what they are. Thus, you will not be able to turn things around and improve on them.

What you really need is qualitative data that can describe and explain why people behave in a certain way. It is not enough to simply know what was sold and what your market share is. You need to know what your target audience thinks about your brand and your product. This allows you to adapt to ensure customer satisfaction and competitiveness. Or as Andrew Chen, a general partner at Andreessen Horowitz, puts it, "If you're not going to do something about it, it may not be worth measuring." To do something about it, you need to know the reasons behind it. Therefore, it is also essential to share data internally. According to a recent study by Brain Consulting, in 40% of cases, individual departments only focus on their own data without any collaboration.

You might think it may be difficult to get your consumers' consent to use their data. Put your mind at ease. Studies have shown that consumers are more than willing to give their data. They just want to know what you are using it for, what benefits they get from it, and whether they can take it back at any time.

Sadly, when it comes to consumer insights, hardly any data is collected.

For a lot of marketers, data management is an ungrateful topic. In contrast to a marketing campaign, results are not seen immediately. Instead of reaping praise, one gets told that this should have been done years ago. Therefore, the topic keeps being postponed. The insights that are used, often stem from third parties and are, thus, outdated and incomplete. Plus, they are prone to error and bias. Let us go through the three most popular data collection methods to explain what I mean.

Market research data is usually collected via online surveys. It does not refer to any specific products and just offers you information on general trends with weak significance. Focus group research is often biased by moderation, setting, and individual character. Since this data always depicts a single moment in the past, it is hard to make quick decisions and react based on it.

Let me put this in perspective for you. If a survey like this is sent to a list of people who have previously registered with the research institute, they are often paid to fill in a questionnaire. They don't necessarily use it or may not have even heard of the product in question before. Therefore, you only get a very general idea of what the population wants and not necessarily what your target audience wants.

Data received from retail partners is also problematic since it is only received weeks or even months after its generation. This data is also only descriptive in nature and does not tell you anything about the how and why of the purchase. On top of that, it makes you dependent on these retailers.

Again, from this kind of data, there is no way to know who bought what and, more importantly, what they thought about the product once in use. It could be that only one person keeps coming back for more. Then, your goal would be to get more people to try the product. Or it could be that a lot of people tried it but then never bought it again. In this case, there might be a problem with the product that needs improving. However, you have no way of finding out since the retailer does not ask these questions.

Even social listening tools are not ideal. These tools will provide real-time data directly from the consumer. However, they put you in the position of a passive listener and observer as you don't have direct access to the consumers. Therefore, it is impossible to respond to them or ask follow-up questions.

Instead, data should be collected first-hand, in real-time, and by using owned sources. Only then will you know how your product is adopted or appropriated in real-life circumstances. It will give you access to detailed information about specific product features, customer expectations, and if those are being met, customer satisfaction, obstacles, likelihood to repurchase as well as the reasons behind the purchase.

Collecting data first-hand can also help you to better define your target audience. Who exactly is buying your products? It allows you to separate data according to region or demographic. This gives you the ability to take local preferences and habits into account and adjust to them. You should also adjust your expectations of life cycle and failure.

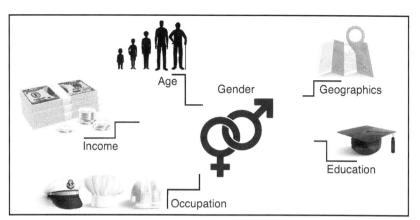

Audience demographics (according to UserReport)

Also, to make the best use of your data, you should make sure to create a single customer view. This basically means that all the data you collect on your customers is stored in one central location and in one single record. This way, you can create an aggregated, consistent, and holistic representation of your customers. This unified view gives you the ability to better analyze past behavior and improve targeting and personalization in future interactions.

You can then use all the data collected and consumer insight taken from it to improve the consumer experience.

Improve Experience

Consumers want their experience to be unique and, most importantly, personal. They want an intimate and individual relationship with their preferred brands, for which they are willing to pay up to 20% more. Digital automation can help achieve this goal not merely by creating personalized content but also through geolocation targeting and the use of AI assistants.

For some long-established companies, this makes it harder to keep up. For other more adaptable brands, this is a great opportunity since they are now able to reach the right kind of people with the right kind of message. In other words, mass channels are losing their appeal, especially for younger generations. In order to reach them, you, as a brand, need to target them directly with highly personalized messages and respond to them in real-time.

That means you also need an efficient way to analyze all the data that is collected—from the feedback received from customer services to all the UGC that is available online. This is a huge amount of data to go through, and it is impossible for one person to do it. Because of this, many brands neglect it. Again, there are software solutions for this.

One incredible example of such a solution is the AI created by DeepOpinion. I talked to the CEO of this young start-up about his motivation and the capabilities of this AI.

Dialogue with Stefan Engl, CEO of DeepOpinion.

What made you decide to start DeepOpinion?
Based on my former entrepreneurial occupation, I realized the incredible value that can be found in qualitative user feedback. You can often find the answers to your brand's challenges and problems by listening closely to your customers. It is, however, next to impossible to analyze a

large quantity of user-generated content manually. For one thing, it takes up way too much time. For another, a person's subjective perception may distort the results.

So, I went in search of a program that could do this. I tried six different vendors, but none could fulfill the task at the level of quality I was expecting. So, I decided to solve this problem myself and build a research team.

So, what exactly is DeepOpinion?

Together with my team, I created an artificial intelligence for opinion mining. To put it simply, it is a software that can read documents, identify relevant topics in them and the tone of voice used by the writer. In other words: What is talked about and how. It turns unstructured text, like UGC, into structured opinion data.

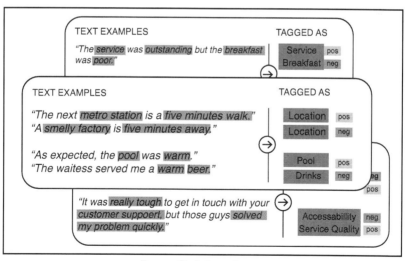

Deep Opinion demo

I need to stress here that DeepOpinion is not a social media monitoring tool. We only provide the core technology.

Such tools are specialized in finding mentions on social media, while we focus on analyzing the collected data. A combination of DeepOpinion with a social media monitoring tool would, thus, offer the best possible analysis and overview of conversations on social media.

What are the benefits for brands?

Consumer insights are incredibly important to brands today. The more you know about your users, the market, and how your products are used, the better decisions you will be able to make in terms of ad-spending, message, channel, product innovation, customer service, etc.

You could, for example, find out which topics are mentioned most often prior to a cancelation or return, thus allowing you to handle these situations more effectively and eventually minimize or even prevent cancelation. Or you could identify all the aspects of a product that are mentioned in its reviews. Based on that, you will know what needs to be changed and what should be communicated more prominently. It also allows for more personalization and thereby makes your customers feel more valued.

The insights found in qualitative feedback are unrivaled. Some brands try to work with market research instead, but that is usually analyzed in some global headquarter and thereby loses all its nuances. Plus, it usually takes forever to get any results.

In today's high-speed world, brands need an effective way to analyze collected data in real-time. DeepOpinion can structure and quantify such qualitative customer feedback. With this, brands can really get to know their consumers.

But don't just believe my word on this. Try it for yourselves. There is a free trial.

> If you are interested in DeepOpinion, you can find more information on our online bonus material: https://www.d2cgrowthrevolution.com/resources# demo

Beliefs vs Actuality

It is time to divide fact from fiction. While many FMCG brands are believed to have already been fully integrated into this new digital age, this is far from accurate.

Most FMCG brands are nowhere near ready to take the step yet. 56% are not equipped to deal with the situation at all. According to a survey conducted by Brain Consulting, 36% of respondents reported insufficient adjustment of IT systems. 30% blamed lack of understanding for the digital transformation, and 28% complain about lack of data management. Only about 28% of companies use a marketing automation system. Evidently, digitization is far out of reach and automation is unthinkable for most.

The brands that have truly arrived in the digital age are very few, only 11%. These proactive brands are forerunners in the field. They leverage the digital to innovate and don't simply use it reactively for small fixes. They are much more prepared to adjust to new technologies. Owned channels are not mere information distribution centers for them; instead, they are used to gather data. These digital brands collect data first-hand via owned channels without relying on others. This way, they know about the upcoming trends, like the increased use of mobile devices, and adapt to them ahead of time by creating mobile apps, for example.

Brands like this do not aim for a mass market—that would only make them one among an endless list of products. Instead, they have used the collected data to personalize and create intimate relationships with their customers.

These are the brands that have realized that an online shop is a viable option for FMCG as well, be it for beauty, household, or food products. This might seem strange to you, but selling food online is the fastest growing e-commerce segment by far at 15.8% p.a. During the corona pandemic, online grocery shopping in the US saw an extraordinary 110% boost in daily online sales in April according to the Adobe Digital Economic Index. In fact, GenZ (16–24) is much more likely to be inspired by and buy via brand owned and social media than from retailers or commercials. This is true for almost half of this age group, 49% according to Wundermann Thompson Commerce.

This is also one of the reasons why start-ups and e-commerce companies are significantly increasing their investments in digital ads while, at the same time, notably decreasing their expenditure on traditional media channels. To be more specific, a 52% increase on Facebook and a 47% rise in Google ads have been coupled with a 27% decrease in print and 26% decrease in TV commercials.

Recap: On + Offline

New trends in this day and age have a big influence on how marketing is done. Digitalization and consumer focus have led to a shift in marketing strategies. This allows for superior consumer intelligence and gives brands the potential to improve their consumer experience.

Even though many are believed to already be taking full advantage of these developments, this is far from accurate. Digital and technological tools have been appropriated but are not yet used to their full potential.

This becomes most apparent when it comes to data collection and use. Data is hardly collected first-hand and mostly descriptive in nature. There is still a major focus on outdated KPIs and not enough focus on regional and demographic nuances. The potential benefit of online recommendations and user-generated content are overlooked and ignored. Brands should use the technology available to them to better communicate with consumers.

The point of this chapter was to explain how the on- and offline worlds are interconnected. The real advantage for brands is that there are tools that can be used to get first-hand, real-time consumer data to adjust and improve their business and marketing models. Also, digitization has made it infinitely easier to manage your brand and products according to the feedback you receive and keep improving. If your brand does not do this, in the best-case scenario, it will miss out on opportunities, and in the worst case, it will leave behind disgruntled customers, ultimately leading to the destruction of the brand.

From digitization, it takes only a small step to achieve total independence. Direct-to-consumer marketing (D2CM) will really set your brand apart from its competition and ensure its long-term success. D2CM allows you to strategically close the gap. This is what we will cover in the next chapter.

7. Direct to Consumer Marketing

You can learn a lot from these brands

"When a company identifies how to integrate the processes needed to give the consumer a sense of job completion, it can blow away the competition. A product is easy to copy, but experiences are very hard to replicate."

—Clayton M. Christensen
Professor of Business Administration
at Harvard Business School

Here is What You Need

By this point, you have surely realized where we are going with this whole argument. Let me lay it out for you. Most FMCG brands are highly reliant and dependent on retail and media agencies. They have no power of their own because they have no direct audience of their own. There is no one to back them up, no one to turn to. Ad campaigns are surrendered to agencies and various channels, product presentations, and customer services are surrendered to retailers and their store personnel.

Get a (Real) Audience

You might disagree with me here and think about your audience on social media. However, even that cannot truly be considered a direct audience since it only enables a superficial kind of interaction. Connecting on social media is not enough to create a real relationship with your consumers. Just like most influencers do not have a real relationship with their followers, neither does a brand. It is next to impossible to target individual consumers directly with this kind of marketing strategy.

In addition to that, organic reach has dramatically reduced and brands have to pay for any kind of communication with customers and brand fans on social media. Circulating messages on social media is expensive. On Facebook, the average CPC is EUR 1.56 and CPM cost around $11.20. That means if you have 10 million followers on Facebook, it will cost you $112,000 to reach all of them.

So, no, you don't have a direct audience. And this fact makes you vulnerable to the whims of others. Actually, relying on retailers and their strategic orientations is becoming increasingly precarious. I mean, just think back to the introduction where we talked about all those brands that are being dropped by retailers and the problems they are facing because of it.

To avoid threats by retailers and regain a solid basis for negotiation, you need the support of your loyal consumers. The customers who really love your brand will simply switch to the retailer that does carry it or, even better, will order directly from you via your online shop. If there is a strong base of advocates, a community supporting you, retailers will have no choice but to list your product. They will not only want to carry it but be required to. Otherwise, they will end up losing valuable customers and their shopping carts.

On the other hand, with direct contact, there is no need to pay for ads to reach your consumers. You can reach out to them directly with individual, personalized messages and create a strong relationship with them. Through continuous value exchange, you bind them to you and increase their CLV.

Two Hemispheres of D2C

Before we get too much into detail, let's make it unmistakably clear what D2C really is. Many still think it merely means selling directly to customers, like through an online shop. However, what it means is cutting out any intermediaries standing between the brands and their consumers. Direct-to-consumer means literally having direct contact with consumers not just in terms of sales but in all aspects. It is about building a direct relationship with consumers. Yes, selling directly to consumers can be a very beneficial part of that for the brand and the consumer because if retailers and other intermediaries are out of the picture, the brand is the only one left to set a price. This will result in a higher profit margin for them. Or if they depend on RSPs (Retail Sales Price), they can have a higher margin to cover the costs of serving directly. Plus, consumers will eventually pay less because there is no third wheel asking for a cut of the earnings.

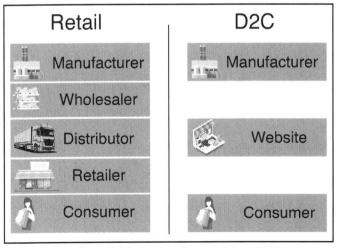

Retail vs D2C (according to Core DNA)

Technical advancement and digitization have not only made this possible, as was mentioned in the previous chapter, but has enormously simplified it. Anyone can set up an online shop nowadays although many traditional brands are still reluctant. They are less agile in adjusting to changing environments and new trends. They may not want to risk their long-established contracts and business relations or might simply be wary of the logistics of it all. However, it is possible even for products with a short expiry date. In fact, the food industry is the fastest-growing sector in terms of e-commerce. Amazon has also started its own food product line and is expanding it. This forces the traditional brands to rethink their current strategy. When it comes to D2C brands directly, in the US, a third of all consumers plan on shopping with D2C brands at least 40% of the time over the next five years. 81% say that they want to shop with one of these brands at least once in that time.

Sales, however, is only one part of D2C. There is also a different aspect of D2C, a second hemisphere. Obviously, I'm referring to marketing—the kind of marketing that does not rely on outdated KPIs, like GRP, but instead, focuses on personalization and the individual. The kind that has the best interest of a brands' consumers at heart.

Direct-to-consumer marketing is about the promotion of products and delivery of brand messages straight from the manufacturer to the consumer.

The advantages of D2C and why and how it should be adapted had been covered by McKinsey in 2017. Today, D2CM allows you to be far less reliant on media agencies.

We have been down this road before. These agencies are incapable of grasping the entirety and the gravity of the current circumstances. They do not see why their traditional way of value creation is no longer working, and this is largely because most of their income stems from brokering ads and commercials in traditional media. They simply do not have the technical know-how to go beyond and fail to see the reasons behind their shortcomings. Because they cannot be objective while giving you the best advice, this leads to an uneven investment in the brand loyalty pyramid.

With D2C, a brand can reach out to its consumers directly without having to rely on others. There is no need to pay for services that are not bringing the desired results. Instead, consumers can be led directly to a brand's owned media by its loyal advocates.

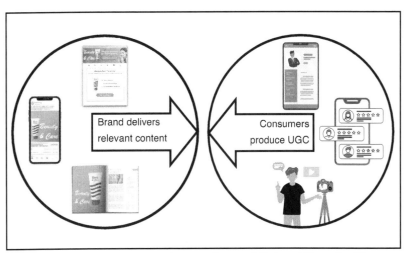

The value exchange (according to Michael Pranikoff)

The basis for the successful execution of D2C is obviously the collection and strategic use of data as we discussed in the previous chapter. Equally indispensable is the possibility of staying in touch with consumers after the sale, which we already know as well. They can give you valuable feedback to help you improve your products and services. They can also supply you with reviews and UGC, such as pictures and videos, which will, in turn, motivate others to try your brands' products.

Look to the Future—Stop Relying on the Past

Instead of relying on an outdated value creation system that largely depends on awareness and reach, brands need to shift their focus towards the individual and their unique needs. Traditional advertising campaigns via mass channels that are aimed at countless people without distinction do not work anymore. The brand loyalty pyramid goes beyond awareness, consideration, and trial. What will really make a difference in today's world and what will set you apart from your competition and ensure sustainable growth cannot be found there. To develop the top two levels of the pyramid— the heavy users and brand advocates—you need to close the gap between awareness and sales uplift. The best way to do so is with a D2C orientation in marketing.

We have already covered the reasons behind this in chapter 1. There are a multitude of advantages that come with it as well.

Advantages of Direct Contact

You can capitalize on direct contact with your consumer. If, after all this, it is still not clear to you why that is something you should want, here are some of the things that this opportunity will make possible for you.

- Direct interaction with your consumers allows you to learn from every encounter with them. Any information you gather can help improve working processes and brand image.

- Consumers appreciate being listened to. If a brand takes their input to heart, these consumers will stay loyal for life.
- You can gain data and consumer insights that would otherwise never be available to you.

- With D2C, you can track customer responses and feedback. What do they like? Who are they? What type of households do they live in?

- You gain valuable consumer insights about product usage, pricing, and messaging.

- You can analyze how consumers perceive your brand first-hand: How do you want people to see your brand and how do they actually see/talk about it? What value is ascribed to your brand? What is the quality of your brand in the eyes of the target audience?

- Tools like DeepOpinion (remember the interview in chapter 6) can help analyze any input related to such questions on a granular level.

- D2C allows you to track the customer decision journey and optimize it for lower acquisition costs as well as higher customer lifetime value.

- It enables you to optimize media spending by building custom or lookalike audiences.

- You can personalize and optimize your messaging based on the collected data.

- By strengthening the relationship between your brand and your consumers, you will gain a competitive edge in a sector that seems to be homogenizing more.

The biggest advantages in D2C lie in the kind of data you are able to collect. Based on all that data and insights, you can improve customer service, offer exactly what your target audience is looking for, adapt quickly to feedback, and so much more.

D2C marketing will help you to establish a strong and loyal fan base for your brand, which can be incorporated in the form of a brand community.

D2C Brand Community

When you decide to take your brand to the future, when you realize the importance of a direct audience and the value of brand advocates, when sustainable growth is what you desire, a brand community should be your next step. So, let's take a look at some of the benefits of a brand community in a new light.

The long-term approach to brand advocacy, building strong relationships, and strategic engagement with consumers cannot be found in traditional advertising. In order to stand out from the increasing amount of ads and brand content that consumers are exposed to every day, personalization and direct relationships are necessary. Relationships that go beyond those on social media can offer this.

Addressing your followers on social media is not free and only lets you distribute another generic message, which will probably go unnoticed anyway since you will be competing with over 50 million business postings on Facebook on a daily basis, only 2% of which achieve organic reach.

What you need is a brand-owned community, a documented personalization strategy like 79% of the brands that exceed revenue goals do. This way, you have full ownership of the consumer relationship with all the benefits mentioned above. On top of this, you will gain the ability to build trust and an emotional connection with consumers, which turns them into loyals because 89% of consumers are loyal to brands that share their values.

Again, to know what these values are, you need data. Collecting first-party data will permit you to deliver customized content. To date, most FMCG brands still don't understand their consumers. They do not even know who these consumers are. They only have a very basic understanding of demographics and purchase history through information that they receive from third parties. This makes creating personalized content very challenging. Without direct contact, there is also no way to deliver it.

A brand-owned community will make it possible to give community members exclusive experiences and the chance to connect with like-minded consumers. You can then engage in a real two-way conversation and incentivize community members to share about your brand, thereby generating more recommendations, and we already know how valuable those are.

An additional major advantage of a brand community is that you have direct access to a forum that is happy to engage with your brand. This means that you can gain some real insight, receive real-time feedback, and test new marketing or product strategies. Most consumers (four out of five) are more than happy to give feedback and enjoy offering input if it helps a brand they love. Acting on received feedback also has the effect of making consumers even more loyal. Moreover, a community can help save up to 25% in customer support costs annually.

The best D2C brands know how to activate brand advocates and make use of the power they hold. Their marketing is focused on social features and community, and they make the best use of consumer recommendations. Traditional brands can learn from this behavior. They should be encouraging their loyal users to share their ideas and content with them and the world.

It might be interesting to find out what kind of consumers are most interested in D2C brands. Research by the IAB UK revealed that these consumers are more likely to influence the purchasing behavior of others. They share more about their own purchases (80%) and are more likely to advise others. 74% stated that people specifically come to them for advice. This is not necessarily just limited to young people. 10% of the participants were 65 years and older. These people are constantly searching for new and interesting things (77%). Plus, this kind of consumer is not very likely to watch TV.

Prime Examples

It is time for some examples. We already know about Tails. com. There are, however, several more outstanding D2C brands out there.

There is Casper, the mattress company. If you are worried about logistics, you should take a look at these geniuses.

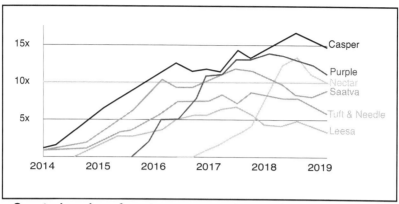

Quarterly sales of mattress companies (by Second Measure)

They managed to devise a way to put mattresses into a box and ship them directly to their consumers' doorsteps for free. Not only that, but they also have a very transparent and generous return policy. It is possible to return a product within 100 days—a feature that distinctly sets them apart from other companies in this sector. This is something they came up with by listening to their consumers' feedback. The brand was included in the club of unicorns within just 5 short years since its launch, which means they are valued at over $1 billion.

You might think there is no comparison here since this is not an FMCG product. Well, here's another one from the personal care sector: The Dollar Shave Club.

Again, this brand offers free shipping directly to its consumers' homes. On top of that, to make the switch from other products easier for prospective customers, they offer a trial set for a ridiculously low price and a thirty-day money-back guarantee. If the customer is happy with the products, refills will be shipped to them at regular intervals.

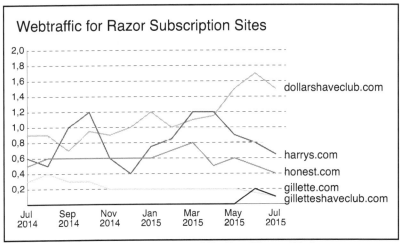

**Soaring success of Dollar Shave Club
(according to Complete)**

This way, the customers never have to worry about going to the store to buy or forgetting to buy ever again. It is a subscription model, but one that is terminable at any time, and it is much cheaper than the traditional brands that are only available in retail stores. The brand launched in 2011, and by 2016, it was acquired by Unilever for $ 1 billion.

There are tons of beauty and make-up brands that had started from a blog or by an influencer. The most famous one is probably Glossier. This D2C brand had a fanbase before it had even launched.

The brand, like all successful D2C brands, is very consumer centric. They listen to the feedback they receive about their products and adjust them accordingly. Also, there is a strong focus on personalization. The brand developed a digital tool that allows consumers to devise the make-up that works best for their individual skin tone. Further, it's not just the products but the packaging also that can be personalized. With every delivery comes a set of stickers to adorn the products with. This incentivizes the consumer to post pictures of the products on social media, leading to tons of UGC the brand can use in their marketing. Not only does this make the consumer feel like a contributing member of the community but it also appears to be much more trustworthy and interesting to other consumers than brand created content. The original blog, Into the Gloss, was launched in 2010, and by 2015, it had 10 million monthly page views and had broadcast the launch of Glossier, the brand. Now, the brand has more than 2.3 million followers on Instagram, and in 2018, it had an annual turnover of more than $100 million.

More brands today are starting their own brand community—not just new and born-digital ones but long-established brands as well, such as LEGO, Nivea, Milka, Jeep, Nike, Manner, and many more.

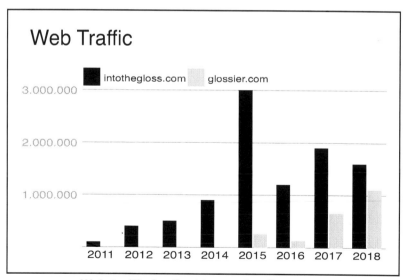

Web traffic for the blog and online store
(according to Rank 2 Traffic)

Maybe the time has come for you to hear what a D2C founder has to say about all this. During the eTail West conference in 2018, Chubbies co-founder Rainer Castillo talked to Yotpo CEO Tomer Tagrin about D2C, brand community, customer centricity, and influencers [paraphrased and shortened].

Interview with Rainer Castillo: Co-founder of Chubbies

Questions by Yotpo CEO Tomer Tagrin

Chubbies is an apparel brand specializing in short shorts for men. It originally started out with four friends designing shorts for a party. The shorts were a hit and they kept getting requests until they decided to turn it into a company and pursue it full time.

Customer Centricity

From day one, we had made those shorts for our friends. Even today, all of Chubbies' communication is like a conversation between friends. It's very important to treat customers like friends. For us, it was the natural thing to do since our customers were our friends from the start. Our creed is: "Customer greater than company, greater than self."

To us, customer contact and customer experience is really important. For example, when we received an email from a customer telling us that his car had been broken into and all his chubbies had been stolen. We replaced his chubbies and gave him karate lessons so it wouldn't happen again. I've learned in previous occupations that being good at selling your product requires you to understand your customers. What do they and don't they want?

We have a lot of feedback loops because if one person has a problem or is excited about something, there may be others who feel the same. That is why we are so reactive to this kind of thing. For example, the leadership team has monthly calls with five customers, focusing on those that have not made a purchase recently. We have one-on-one conversations with them and broadly distribute what we have learned.

Or we also have a post-purchase survey. If someone puts forth the effort to send you an email, you definitely need to read, react, and respond to it. This is "somebody who cares enough to say something."

We have received feedback from a customer who said the 5 ½" shorts is just too short for someone who is 6'5". So, we developed 7-inch shorts. This kind of connection builds so much trust and loyalty. We have people specifically tasked to make sure that the consumer's voice is always central to our operation. It is in our DNA.

Community and Ambassadors

We have a loyalty program to retain our community. They receive gifts based on their purchasing behavior. We have events for our most loyal customers and biggest advocates. There, they receive special gifts with every purchase.

Then, there is our ambassador program. In the early days of the brand, I had mailed leaders on college campuses, sports team captains, or presidents of student groups. I had told them about our brand and asked if they knew someone who could represent us on campus.

That program became a core of our business. We have active conversations with them. They vote for the next products that should come out. We have had photo challenges and they would provide content for our Instagram posts and campaigns. "It was never a sales mechanism; it was always part of the community." Our content is ideally from the community and for the community. It's not a sales message, but on its own, it's really enjoyable.

Building a community starts by talking with a customer. There are people out there who are passionate about your product. You have to find those advocates who love that piece of your brand and then focus and make sure to build on it.

Influencer Marketing
For us, it happens organically. One of our customers, for example, happened to be on a season of The Bachelorette. He got in touch with us to get some shorts to wear on the show. We were on ABC prime-time TV for weeks without doing anything except provide a few shorts.

Our ambassadors are reflective of our most loyal customers and biggest advocates. They are living, breathing, walking, and talking interpretations of the brand.

One of our interns had seeded some of our products with people who had a lot of followers once. However, it didn't feel natural. It didn't make sense. It felt forced. Being authentic is important.

Recap: High Time to Start

It is now or never. Direct-to-Consumer brands are disrupting and overhauling the marketing scene. They do this by creating a relationship that consumers want to talk about with their peers. D2C brands' experience-driven product strategy is restraining the growth of the biggest players.

These traditional brands are facing increasing pressure from all sides. TV and other mass channels' audiences are dwindling. Social media gardens are raising their walls and keeping their information under lock and key. Retailers are increasing their demands; they want higher margins but offer less desirable shelf spaces. On top of that, consumers are losing interest in brand messages and have higher expectations for brands. This is a contest that cannot be won by increasing advertising pressure.

You cannot buy audiences. You have to build them by winning, developing, binding and activating brand advocates. Close the gap between awareness and sales uplift strategically and efficiently. Stop relying on third-party platforms to do it for you.

Traditional marketing is impersonal because it is done on a large scale. Direct marketing techniques allow for more personalization and intimacy. Stop focusing on building awareness with a new customer; D2C marketing puts you in contact with people who already want what you have to provide. Don't waste time on those who might not want your product; concentrate on the people who are really interested by following the example of Chubbies.

Invest in D2C strategies and take control of the available data and the entire customer decision journey because loyal users and brand advocates are the secrets to sustainable growth and long-term success. Cut out any unnecessary intermediaries between you and your consumers to become more independent and self-sufficient. Then, you will automatically become more appealing to retailers and ensure your spot on their shelves.

Consumers' demands have changed. In order to stay relevant to them and secure your audience, you need to adjust. There is a new way to brand growth, which we will discuss in the next chapter.

8. New Way for Brands to Grow

Combining the new and the old

to cover all bases

"A brand is the set of expectations, memories, stories, and relationships that, taken together, account for a consumer's decision to choose one product or service over another."
—Seth Godin
Author of 19 best-selling books

"We Don't get them to try our product by convincing them to love our brand; we get them to love our brand by convincing them to try our product."
—Bob Hoffman
Creator of The Ad Contrarian

Rundown

We have arrived at the last chapter. A lot has been discussed until now. A lot has been learned. Hopefully, some eyes have been opened and perspectives have changed. We are, however, not quite done yet. There is still more to come. One last all-encompassing argument has to be made. So don't put the book aside just yet. The last thing I want to show you as you go on your way is the new way to grow consistently and sustainably. A way to put everything that has been discussed in the book so far to good use. A way to combine the old and the new.

Why the Old Way is Not Enough

The original brand value creation model is insufficient in today's day and age. New trends have developed that require new methods and strategies.

Consumers are not what they used to be. New generations of young consumers have different needs and expectations about brands. Advertisements on mass channels are less likely to reach them. They have moved away from the TV and onto streaming services. Now, people generally have a very different outlook towards the world and their lives. They are looking to live healthier and be more environment friendly. They want to buy from brands that share these values. One of the most important values today is trust. There has been too much twisting the truth in the past and too much greenwashing. Today, consumers intentionally block out advertisements, and tons of sources are easily available that allow consumers to separate fact from fiction. Advertisements and brand messages are no longer trusted. What we all do believe in, however, are our friends and authentic online resources like product reviews.

Changing channels and technologies have enabled consumers to get in touch with each other. We are now able to talk to actual brand users and get real testimonies. New channels have also enabled consumers to get in touch with the brand directly. We now expect personalized content from the sites we visit regularly and real two-way communication. This, in turn, creates an opportunity for brands to get more detailed data in real-time. On the other hand, this means that it is not possible to reach everyone via one all-encompassing channel anymore. The media landscape has become fragmented. A multitude of different channels and platforms are available today, and audiences are scattered across them all. Consumers want brands to simplify their lives for them. They want to be able to go from a picture on social media directly to the online shop, preferably to the checkout page. They don't want to have to personally go to different retail stores and try to find one that carries the product they are looking for.

The market itself has changed as well. New brands are popping up left and right and catering to hyper-focused niches instead of focusing on a mass audience. Retailers are also facing more pressure from discounters' low prices; the comfort, simplicity, and accessibility of online shops and their home delivery; and from consumers and their demands.

Retailers have realized that brand loyalty is declining and are taking advantage of that fact by introducing more in-house brands and demanding lower prices and higher margins from traditional brands. Relationships between brands and consumers are becoming increasingly fragile and strained. Media agencies fail to take all these trends into account and, thus, are unable to counsel brands properly.

In short, a long-established brand name and message released onto mass markets is not enough to catch consumer's interest anymore. Merely raising awareness will get a brand nowhere in this day and age.

A Healthy Brand

Only a healthy brand can survive in this turbulent environment. Something more than awareness is needed to hold people's interest.

The brand triad has made it evident that this "something more" is sympathy. Only the brand that consumers can really relate to will be eligible for a trial. If not, the consumers will find it pointless to switch from a brand they already use and are satisfied with. Only an emotional bond can combat the problems caused by market saturation and increasing ad pressure.

Health goes beyond this, however. The brand loyalty pyramid illustrates that first-time users or consumers in the trial stage are not responsible for the bulk of a brand's profit. They never will be. They can't be. Since acquisition costs are typically much higher than any revenue or profits made off first-time purchases to so-called trialists. Even regular customers are still highly likely to switch to other brands. Thus, brands need to turn their users into loyals and advocates.

Loyal users are the basis for a healthy and successful brand. They are the consumers any brand dreams of. However, only loyalty based on an emotional bond will last. The best way to create such a connection with your consumers is a brand community. A community gives a brand direct access to feedback, a forum, a discussion board, and product testers as well as people to test new strategies on.

These consumers are responsible for 80% of the profits, even if they only make up 20% of the consumer base. Therefore, you should generate more of them. In addition to that, they are the best and most reliable way to create more consumers for a brand. These advocates are trusted by their peer group and, thus, the ideal addition and catalyst to any marketing strategy. Best of all, they do not require any incentive to recommend your products to others. They will simply do so because they love your brand. The only thing you as a brand need to do is activate the 90% of advocates that are currently inactive. These are the people who are happy to engage with your brand or, in other words, the ultimate embodiment of the D2C principle.

Consumer Decision Journey Mapping

To convince people of the superiority of a product, you need to get them to try it. Mapping out the consumer decision journey helps you understand how they make their choices and how this can be influenced by brands.

The journey always starts with a trigger—a specific situation that lets people think about buying a certain kind of product or something that immediately brings several brands to mind. This initial consideration then evolves into active evaluation. Here, people actively look for information on what to get and where, which is a crucial point for any brand. If they are not represented in this phase and if their information is not easily accessible, they are very likely to lose consumers to the competition. This means it is necessary to offer simple and relevant information as well as authentic product ratings on all kinds of media. Only then can consumers form a complete and authentic picture of your brand and product and decide based on this information whether to prefer your brand as opposed to others. In order to create the coveted loyal consumer, you also need to ensure a gratifying post-purchase experience. Entice consumers to become loyal, maybe even an advocate, so that they can go on to become the trigger for another consumer's decision journey.

A more consumer-centric focus in marketing and business will ensure an increase in advocates and, thereby, recommendations.

Recommendations Combine Reach and Trust

Recommendations are a sign of good brand performance. By tracking your Net Promoter Score, which correlates with brand success, you can measure your performance and compare it to the competition and the market. Remember, NPS leaders profit from four times the growth rate of brands with low scores.

If a recommendation is made by a person you trust, the trust will transfer to the products recommended. Recommendations are authentic, highly personalized, and not pushed onto you when you do not need or want them. They are the perfect advertisement. With today's technical advancements, all of this can not only be accelerated but tracked and analyzed.

Digital Possibilities

Technical innovation is happening so fast and diversely that many brands can't keep up. Digital advancement is causing the on- and offline worlds to blur. Among other things, recommendations do not necessarily have to happen solely offline anymore. Word of mouth can spread online much faster and much farther than ever before. This can be tracked by brands and even used in their marketing. Anything created by consumers, from product ratings to user-generated content like pictures, increases the trustworthiness of brands.

Since almost everything we do today happens online, it can all be turned into data, which is something many brands are still not taking full advantage of. First-party data is of inescapable importance today. Consumer insights can help you improve your product, marketing, targeting, and much more. Most importantly, it gives you the ability to make informed decisions based on the collected data.

Combat the Trends Disrupting the Original Value Creation Model

Direct relationships with consumers are essential if a brand wants to survive and grow sustainably. Direct-to-consumer sales and marketing help you do just that. It cuts out intermediaries from this strained relationship and strengthens the emotional bond between the brand and the consumer. It helps brands create a real, direct audience—a very important asset when it comes to negotiations with retailers. The brand's audiences, fans, loyals, and advocates are the ones who ensure the brand's success.

D2C allows brands to get in touch with all their brand loyals and advocates without having to pay for advertisements that might not ever even reach them. With D2C strategies in place, brands are capable of collecting the data that is so essential to their success.

By now, you might be thinking where the new addition is. We heard all of this before. Well, yes. You are right. I wanted to refresh your memory because it is a compilation of all this that makes up the new way for brands to grow. It is a combination of all these new developments with the old methods that will really allow traditional brands to survive the 21st century and grow sustainably.

New Growth Model

The old approach of "publish and pray" is no longer an option. Today, traditional methods need to be complemented with a D2C approach to successfully close the gap between awareness and sales uplift. A strategy that focuses on increasing reach and ad pressure does not ensure the sales of products any longer. Consumers don't usually transform into loyal users or brand advocates on their own. This most crucial part of the customer decision journey has been left up to chance for far too long. To ensure the growth of your brand, you need to make it easy for consumers to adopt your brand.

Due to channel fragmentation and media surplus, it is getting harder to reach consumers. We have to make them curious, entice them away from the competition, and give them the necessary information to convince them.

As you can imagine, it is next to impossible to incorporate all of this in classical media. If, for example, a brand manager now tries to launch a product simply through a TV or digital campaign, it typically runs into a dead end.

The customer journey will end again after such a passive ad impression. The attention of the target audience—if it was ever there—will shift to the next ad or be drowned by one of the thousands of other impressions. It is obvious that this ad impression will have a considerably small impact on any potential purchase decision.

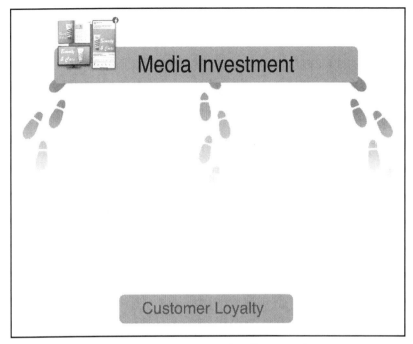

Media investments are leading nowhere

Why make it easy when it can be so complicated? Why continue to have dead-ends in advertisement and not use the possibilities digitization has given us and use ad impressions as a starting point for a brand owned journey?

A consumer journey that does not only draw my target audience's full attention but also controls all the information gives me, as a brand, complete data sovereignty. It allows me to simplify and simultaneously increase the conversion between the steps of their journey.

Yes! This is a viable option for FMCG brands, even the ones without an online shop.

Just think about how successful companies like Netflix and Spotify do it. These companies understand that half the battle is won if they know who is interested in their service. They connect to and collect valuable data about all their prospects. They offer a free trial and a convincing product experience to their target audience, thereby turning anonymous web traffic into real people with names, contact information, and serious enthusiasm for what they offer.

Many of you might wonder which parallels can be drawn from such services to physical products. You might think that this is impracticable and cannot work for your industry.

Yet, believe me, the opposite is the case.

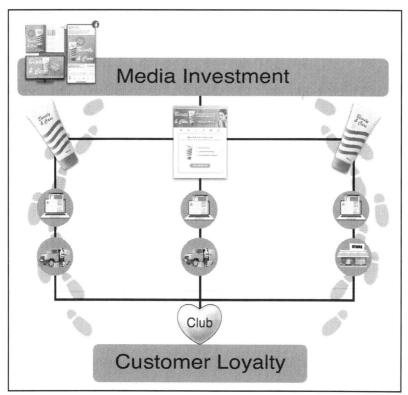

Fully controlled customer journey

By simply incorporating a call to action like "free trials now!" into your next media campaign, you can connect it to a D2C campaign and lead tens of thousands of consumers directly to your owned media channels like I have done for dozens of brands already. This way, any uncertainties about signing up or purchasing new products are eliminated. Any advertisement will become more efficient in this way, and the likelihood of further interaction will increase immensely. Thus, you can connect to your target audience, begin to bridge the gap between awareness and sales uplift, build an end-to-end consumer journey, and try to continue the story from there.

Such a call to action will trigger the interest of users and animate them to interact with your brand beyond the passive recognition of an advertisement. It will lead interested parties to your website and initiate an in-depth examination of the brand and the product. During this part, it is incredibly important to have a good and authentic story—one that captivates the reader and sells credibly step by step.

Once your potential users are on your website, they can immerse themselves completely into your brand environment. Here, you have their full attention. They have taken a step towards you and want to know more about your brand and product. Most importantly, you have caved a clear next step for the user to follow in their customer decision journey—a free trial. This results in much higher performance and less churn along every step of the way. In other words, the awareness generated this way considerably surpasses the one originating solely from any paid media campaigns. D2C marketing can make traditional marketing strategies infinitely more effective.

To receive the free trial, participants will sign up, which means they will willingly give you their data, names, address, and additional information you require, allowing you to identify and activate a specific target group of ideal users. You then give free trials exclusively to the ones most likely to become heavy users and brand advocates. All of this makes it much easier for you to target the right people from the get-go next time.

With this method, you increase awareness as well as engagement for your brand. A campaign like this will familiarize participants with your product, establish an emotional connection, and systematically activate them for your marketing. This will effectively close the gap between awareness and sales uplift. The data collected in the process will also enable you to form valuable audiences for targeting and retargeting campaigns.

Further, you can activate this audience to help you reach your specific goals. Do you want them to write an authentic review of your product? Ask them. Do you want to gain consumer insights? Ask them. Do you want them to spread the word about your product among their peers? Ask them.

An average of 83% of participants in this kind of D2C campaign will remain loyal brand users afterward. They will share this experience with their friends, thereby creating authentic and trustworthy reach on- and offline.

UGC created throughout the trial period of such campaigns can then be used for product reviews on relevant online touchpoints, marketing figures, claims, testimonials, images, etc. This will also provide you with invaluable consumer insights and data to help you improve your brand and business decisions.

With a campaign like this, the touchpoints will multiply and intensify. Your brand will appear to be more approachable, trustworthy, and credible. This will aid in the purchasing decisions of future customers. Newly released products will sell faster and better. Customers will keep coming back and recommend their friends, thereby boosting your growth and shrinking your costs.

This example shows what you need to continually acquire new user for your brand. But what about turning them and existing brand users into loyal advocates? To solve that challenge, we'll take a look at creating a brand community so that you can turn your brand's growth efforts into a flourishing flywheel.

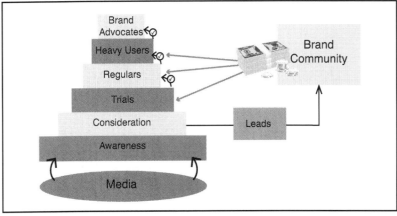

Systematic growth with a brand community

By creating a brand community, you efficiently tie your most loyal consumer to your brand. This grants you constant direct access to them. Whenever you need to generate reviews, recommendations, or UGC, these advocates are just a click away. Community members can help you explain products to new users and minimize obstacles for them. Best of all, compared to communication on social media or other third-party channels, communication via owned media is free. There is no need to rely on generic messages via a mass channel and no EdgeRank to limit your organic reach. Instead, you are able to send direct and personalized messages to individual consumers. For example, if a customer has not purchased anything in a while, send them a 10% discount coupon to get them back.

Therefore, a brand community is also the perfect place to kickstart any product launch. Simply announce the launch to your brand community by sending a message to your brand users, loyal fans, and community members. Reaching out to your loyal fans and heavy users could not be easier or more cost-effective. Additionally, by offering them the exclusive chance to be among the first to try your new product, you will push initial sales and trigger word of mouth right from the start. This is when the flywheel starts to spin.

From "Publish and Pray" to an Ever-Spinning Flywheel

Use media to increase awareness and take consumers to the first micro-conversion: signing-up for the chance to receive a free trial. Segment all sign-ups to identify your ideal brand users and activate them within a D2C campaign. Create an outstanding brand experience. Educate consumers, strengthen the brand–customer relationship, and finally, convert new brand users. Tie them to your brand in your brand community. Reward them for their loyalty and increase customer retention. Turn loyal brand users into brand advocates and activate them to spread the word.

Start over again: Use media to increase awareness and take consumers.

I hope you got it. This is exactly what you should aim for in today's marketing scenario. Drop the obsolete publish and pray approach in marketing and replace it with a spinning flywheel that fuels scalable brand growth and maximizes the efficiency of every advertising dollar spent.

Having said this, let me take you through the very last model in this book to show you how the brand loyalty pyramid turns into the flywheel.

AARRR

The pirate metrics or AARRR framework is one that many growth hackers have been building fabulous startups upon.

A—Acquisition
A—Activation
R—Revenue
R—Retention
R—Referral

A—Acquisition
How and where do customers find my brand?

This stage really doesn't change all that much. Obviously, the most common source for consumers' awareness of your brand is still media. But instead of shouting generic brand messages and just hoping for the best, we are going to open a funnel and lead customers to the next stage, the second "A."

A—Activation
How can I create an outstanding first experience for potential brand users? How can I activate them accordingly? How can I get them closer to my brand?

This is where the journey continues and D2C marketing campaigns enter the playing field. By offering free trials, you create an effective onboarding process and turn your anonymous target audience into individuals with names, email addresses, and much more. By creating a transparent consumer journey, you make it easy for consumers to move from being a passive listener to an active prospect interested in your brand. Creating an extraordinary experience for these consumers converts them to brand users.

R—Revenue
How to earn and increase revenue?

Implementing what is stated above will undoubtedly turn cold traffic into new brand users and earn first revenue for your brand. However, as we know by now, you cannot build your FMCG brand on first-time buyers. Your loyal customers will always be responsible for the bulk of your profit. This is why you should concentrate on building retention from the start.

Having collected tons of customer data, start thinking about further monetization strategies. Could opening an online shop instead of relying solely on traditional retailers be worth it?

R—Retention
How can I turn first time brand users to loyal customers? How can I increase retention and loyalty?

First, create a product that customers truly love. Having said that, giving your customers a voice and honoring them with appreciation will lead to the development of a strong connection between your brand and customers. This is easier said than done. Nonetheless, a brand community is a perfect place to do so. With constant direct access to your customers, you can start integrating them into your decision making. Let them be the first to give feedback on new concepts, create exclusive benefits for them, or invite them to participate in your launch campaigns and have them spread the word. By doing so, you will be able to build a strong emotional connection with your customers and maximize retention and loyalty. On the other hand, insights taken from these relationships can, in turn, be used to optimize products, brand messaging, and market position.

R—Referral

How can you turn your customers into your advocates?

This is probably the easiest step along the journey. Simply ask your existing loyal brand users and community members to refer you to their friends and family. Start campaigns within your brand community to leverage your brand users' voices to spread the word. Incentivize them, provide them with free samples, and ask them. They will be happy to share samples with their peers, invite friends, produce content, and spread the word across social media, thus helping you to further recruit new brand users.

Now that you know the AARRR framework as well as the traditional brand pyramid, you know exactly how to put all this theory into action for your brand. You know now why you have to drop the traditional publish and pray approach and instead turn to this new D2C growth revolution.

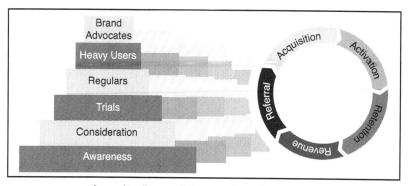

Loyalty Pyramid turns into Flywheel

After aligning the AARRR model with the steps of the brand pyramid, it should be crystal clear how to bridge the gap between awareness and sales uplift and turn all this into a flywheel, an ever-growing system to recruit, retain, and activate brand users.

Sounds simple enough, right? So, go ahead and do it. If you need help, shoot me an email: hello@d2cgrowthrevolution.com

Recap: This is it!

We have reached the end of this book. So, it is time to reveal to you the key takeaways and how to combine everything that has been discussed so far in order to create a new and sustainable way to grow. As I had highlighted many times throughout the book, what you are doing now is not wrong; it is simply not enough. The solution, the way into the future, is a combination of the old and the new.

Declining growth rates predict the fast-approaching death of longstanding FMCG brands. Retailers are putting pressure on them as are the increasing numbers of new players.

Break free from your dependence on retailers and other intermediaries. Make sure your customers are the only thing you are dependent on. This way, retailers' success becomes dependent on you. Brands need to adjust to a new, genuinely consumer-centric orientation in order to close the gap between awareness and sales uplift. In this thoroughly saturated market, relying on ad pressure alone is not going to do the trick. We need to appeal to our consumers on a different level, a deeper one, an emotional level.

The frameworks and methods I introduced in this book are proven. It is time for you to change your marketing game and to join the D2C growth revolution.

About the Author

STEFAN RAMERSHOVEN is a Growth Marketer, Digital Expert, and co-founder of several companies. Among others, Kjero. He founded the company while still in University and has been running it successfully as CEO for almost a decade. Working in cooperation with some of the world's leading CPG and Consumer Electronics brands (Nestlé, Henkel, Beiersdorf, Wilkinson, Mars, Melitta, Dr. Oetker, Bosch, Philips...). Today Kjero is one of the leading providers for direct-2-consumer marketing solutions. He was mentioned in several publications, books, and as one of Forbes 30 under 30.

RESOURCES

- Bonus Chapter

- Resource Pack

- DeepOpinion Demo

- Volvo Interception

- Generic Brand Video

- Bibliography

All recouces, bonus materials and a bibliography can be found online:
https://www.d2cgrowthrevolution.com/recourses

Printed in Great Britain
by Amazon

79018562R00121